THE
NEW
AGE
A to Z

THE NEW AGE
A TO Z
(x - ept x!)

A Dictionary

by
GARI GOLD

Published by ZIVAH Publishers

Zivah Publishers Phoenix, AZ 85044
Zivah Publishers Albuquerque, NM 87192

©1991 by Gari Gold

13 12 11 10 9 8 7 6 5 4 3 2

Cover design by Peter Pauley

Publisher's Cataloging in Publication Data

Gold, Gari, 1953-
   The New Age A to Z (x - ept x!): a dictionary /
   by Gari Gold

   p. cm.
   Includes bibliographical references.

   1. New Age movement - Dictionaries. I. Title.

BP605.N48G6   1992   299.93
                            QB191-2017

LCCCN 91-68566

ISBN 0-9622707-6-8

∞

The following compilation of terms should not be understood as an endorsement of any particular healing method or philosophy.

When considering care for any health problem, competent health care professionals should be consulted and an appropriate course of medical treatment or therapy should be pursued.

Philosophies and ideas presented here are offered as points of view and not as facts.

about the author

Gari Gold resides in Sedona, Arizona where she
carries on her many and varied interests. She is
a student and teacher of hatha yoga, a dancer
and teacher of dance as well as a gem therapist
and a writer. Gari's activities give her an
opportunity to meet many people who are discovering New Age. It is out of these meetings
that she recognized a need for this book.

acknowledgments

Special thanks to the many people who helped in the creation of this book through their willingness to share information from their libraries and in their fields of expertise. Thanks especially to Tony Locane and to John Nekritz for extensive discussion of material included in the book. Thanks also to Zivah for their confidence in my work and for their vision of the New Age.

*dedicated to
the memory of
my father*

Welcome to the "New Age!"

How many times did you hear the expression "New Age" before you started to say "hey, I've heard that before." Yet you still didn't really know what it meant? Now you may have heard it so many times, you might even be embarrassed to ask what it means. At first it was OK not to understand the New Age. After all, it was just kooks and weirdos who were involved in it. Who needed to know about that anyway when there were so many real things to think about? Then you kept hearing about "meditation" and "psychic healers" and "crystals." And strangely enough, people you knew and respected, famous people, important people, movers and shakers on the planet, were getting involved in this New Age business. It was getting coverage on television and in magazines. It was beginning to gain some credibility. So now it's time to ask how this all fits together and what it might mean in your own life.

You are the only one who can know what the ideas loosely gathered under the umbrella of "New Age" will mean in your life. Before you wholeheartedly embrace this philosophy, you might like a better understanding of what "New Age" means and how it can affect your life.

The New Age A to Z is a dictionary of the principles, ideas and techniques of New Age philosophy. It is beyond the scope of this book to present an in depth discussion of each word and phrase found here; however, there is enough information to make it easy to do more research on any topic which interests you and causes you to want to pursue it in more depth.

Since questioning existing philosophies and institutions is one of the characteristics of New Age people, let's start out by questioning the New Age itself. The first question to be asked is: Is it really "new?" Maybe the New Age would be easier to grasp if it were called the "next age" or the "new understanding." The New Age is a blending of many philosophies from various parts of the world and various eras of human development. This blending of ideas is a result of our desire to understand ourselves at a deeper level than we have in the past. It also reflects a disillusionment with the traditional methods of looking for that understanding.

The influence of the New Age can be seen in the field of music, in health care, in our concern for the ecology, in our pursuit of progressive and alternative life styles and in our study of the supernatural or paranormal aspects of life. Its impact is most noticeable in western Europe, Australia and North America.

But back to our original question - how much of this is really new? I suppose the answer is none of it and all of it. Although very appropriate for today, many New Age ideas are rooted in some very old concepts, but New Age thought is selective. It chooses and tests these ideas for validity in this time and this culture. Innovation, assimilation and modification, all hallmarks of progressive thought and action, are being reintroduced into our culture by the New Age. For example, hypnosis, formerly considered a parlor game, is now being used successfully by medical doctors to stop pain and help patients find reasons for disturbances which have been locked away from their conscious memory for many years. It is also used to help people quit smoking, lose weight and release other addictive and destructive behaviors.

For a number of years, science has been investigating the more difficult to understand aspects of our psyches. In many cases, the motivation behind some of the investigation may have been to destroy belief in charlatans and others who sell hocus pocus. However, the true scientists, those who investigated with open minds, have discovered some surprising results from their studies in areas such as herbology, hypnosis, meditation and acupuncture.

As an example, through experimentation with acupuncture, an ancient Chinese healing method in use for thousands of years, modern science is learning more about the natural ability of the body to protect and heal itself. In experimental surgeries, doctors have used acupuncture instead of chemical pain killers or anesthesia to relieve pain. There have been numerous successes and medical doctors have come to feel that acupuncture is useful and safe in certain types of surgery. As a result of these kinds of studies, our knowledge of the human body and its functions as previously taught and accepted by our western medical profession is being seriously challenged.

The next question we'll ask is: Are we really in a New Age or is that phrase just another advertising gimmick calculated to sell us something? Let's take a quick trip back through history to get a broader look at where we have been, where we are and where we are going. It is clear that life on earth is very different than it was 1000 years ago, even different than it was

200 years ago. More recently, the leap we have taken off the planet has changed life in a significant way. We now know for certain that God is not sitting up above the earth on a cloud and it has been a long time since very many of us hunted or farmed as our ancestors did. At best we hunt for packages in fluorescent forests then "nuke" our food in minutes. Health care is handled differently. We look to well-trained, specialized health professionals who treat only one small part of the body, instead of being nursed and nurtured by family members or perhaps treated by one doctor who has watched over us since birth.

Our technology has benefitted us in many ways. The products of our industry have afforded many of us freedom from difficult labor or repetitive tasks and we enjoy a higher quality of life, in some respects, than was possible in the small, isolated farming communities which used to make up much of our world. In the last 50 years medical science has found treatments for diseases that previously killed great numbers of people. We take certain routine surgical procedures, dental and eye care somewhat for granted. We live longer, have more leisure time and are more educated and sophisticated than ever before.

So, in view of all that's happened, are humans intrinsically different today? No, not really. Our life styles may be different but we are fundamentally the same people we were 200 years ago. Because of that, many of the changes we have undergone have stressed our bodies, our minds and our deeper psyches in ways we could not have anticipated. Our urbanized lifestyles have disconnected us from nature and from each other. Fortunately, we can still find these connections to nature and to each other in our myths and stories. They tell us in a symbolic way of our origins and our relationship to each other and to the universe. Myths also tell of our place in the material world and of our inner workings. As fantastic as myths can be, they speak clearly to our deeper nature in a mysterious and undefined way.

Myths from around the world and from different time periods share many similarities. For example, biblical, Egyptian and Native American myths which describe the creation of life do so in much the same way, uniting us at a basic level as human beings.

Throughout history, and everywhere on the planet, people have had a need to make sense of their existence. The myths about birth, death and what goes on in between speak to a part of every human being who has taken a breath and wondered how and why. We have not changed really. We have grown. Grown and evolved. And we will continue to evolve for all eternity.

As we look back through prehistory and history, we see that archaeologists and historians have named many "ages:" the Ice Age, the Stone Age, and more recently the Industrial Age. These are all names given to large blocks of time in our history when important changes in geology or culture took place. Most of these "ages" were so named after the fact. They weren't recognized for what they were while they were happening. Now, however, we have entered a more self-conscious time. We are more aware of what is happening to us as it happens. Perhaps this is a function of our ability to communicate with each other more quickly than we could in the past. We actually recognize the profound changes that we must make and are making because our world condition demands it. We call this age the "New Age."

And now to answer our question. No, the New Age is not selling anything. However, it does offer us ways to improve our quality of life. It does this differently than the Bronze or the Industrial Age did. The New Age gives us a different kind of tool. Instead of a knife or a machine which can help us make something in the world outside our own psyche, New Age tools help us to improve our lives by gaining a different perspective with which to understand ourselves, each other and our relationship to the world we live in. And no money need ever change hands for this shift to occur.

The next question we can ask is: Why does the New Age seem to reach to places and times other than the here and now for its answers? And, what do old myths and other cultures have to do with today or the future in our own culture? To answer that question, let's take a look at our advanced society. Crime, drug abuse, depression, broken families, pollution of our environment are symptoms of the malfunctioning of our culture. All of our industrial and technical advances have failed to nurture us toward a healthy maturity either as individuals or as a society.

It has become necessary for us to stop, look, and repair the damage. Perhaps there was something we knew when we lived closer to nature and have now forgotten. The old stories, our myths, are our greatest direct link to understanding ourselves in that state of being. Tapping into the old stories doesn't mean that we have to live as if we had gone back in time. New Agers are picking up the threads of thought spun by the ancient sages, prophets, teachers, healers and mystics and available to us through myth and story. And the hope is that these strong, old threads can be woven into the fabric of modern life. The New Age is not about turning back the clock to ancient times or living like some other culture. It is about using the best of available knowledge to make us healthier, happier and more creative as individuals and as members of a planetary being.

So if the New Age wants to reach to the old stories and myths and lifestyles, is there any room for all the scientific development occurring today? Of course there is. New Age thought also seeks to integrate the theories of modern science into our lives. We no longer function in an environment which supports the concept of a purely mechanized world. In that world, computers would be an impossibility. Also impossible would be the psychic phenomena experienced by so many people today that we can no longer call them crazy and dismiss them as having no relevance in our lives. Science and medicine are now recognizing the mind-body connection as a giant breakthrough to better health care. The origins of many "new" concepts can be found in old sayings, old wives tales and old teachings. Now, however, many of these old concepts have been validated by modern scientific observation.

Those on the cutting edge of the advanced physical sciences are finding that the ambiguous statements and seemingly chaotic, maze-like answers of the Zen masters and mystics, were actually conveying a more accurate and in-depth picture of the universe than any scientist might have realized 50 years ago. What is wonderful is not that we are finding the scientific validation of this ancient wisdom, but that we have even looked there for our answers.

Our lifestyles have changed over the years but our questions as humans have changed very little. By going forward with our scientific studies we have come full circle; we have returned to our ancient wisdom and to the old questions with a greater knowledge, and thus with a greater potential to gain wisdom from their answers. The New Age is blending modern and ancient, science and story and, in doing so, is creating new myths for our times.

But how does one know that the New Age is here to stay? Every important advance in a culture is heralded by changes in all areas of that culture. Every true cultural movement is supported by individuals in all the disciplines which together make up a culture: 1) architecture, 2) fine arts: sculpture, painting, 3) music, 4) literature, 5) science, medicine, 6) religion. Indeed, today there are New Age ideas at work in all of these areas.

In architecture, geodesic domes, solar energy panels and homes made entirely of recycled materials are changing the look of neighborhoods.

New Age art is called "visionary." Using a narrative or story telling style in painting, it is the ideas represented in visionary painting that link these works of art to the New Age.

There is a new and ever expanding music category, "New Age music." No longer just a small underground movement, the New Age music market has captured millions of dollars worth of business and is still growing. As of this writing (early 1992), some statistics indicate that the sales of New Age recordings have surpassed those of jazz.

Literature has taken a new turn with all of the "channeled" books and underground material available. On a more mundane, practical level, self improvement books have never been more popular. Periodicals are our way of keeping up to the minute with information in all areas of life and there are hundreds of magazines directed at special interest groups related to New Age thought.

In the realm of science and medicine a spectacular number of advances has been made. These advances have changed how our phone services work, how we cook, clean, bank and dress. The technological advances of science have changed the face of medicine forever and in turn medicine has been provided with a broad spectrum of new approaches to old problems.

Religion probably takes the limelight with its highly visible and often controversial New Age philosophies. New churches have been formed - some offshoots of traditional churches, some founded on nontraditional beliefs.

Who and what belongs to the New Age, you ask? Well, there is no entrance exam and no panel of peers to answer to. There are no by-laws to uphold and no membership fees. The New Age is a state of mind and members of the New Age are generally self-proclaimed. There are as many reasons to gravitate to the New Age as there are philosophies which make it up.

However, sometimes those who believe, practice and even teach New Age ideas and techniques, do not want to be considered a part of the New Age. They may not agree or wish to be associated with all others who consider themselves New Age. Unfortunately, in all good barrels of apples, there are a few bad ones. So it is with the New Age. In fact there may even be a few barrels that aren't so good. In all "movements" there are con artists, and shysters. There are those who are misinformed and those who are fanatics. There are those who will latch onto any group - the New Age, the anti-New Age, abortion, anti-abortion - simply to find an identity for themselves and to give themselves the opportunities they need for their survival, be it social, emotional or monetary. These are the ones that give the New Age, or any group, a bad reputation. This is unfortunate and unavoidable. It is human nature for some to be opportunists, some to misuse, misunderstand or be misled in any undertaking. And this in no way negates the philosophy in general.

It may sound as if there are no definite rules to the New Age. It might even be confusing and difficult to decide whether the New Age and its ideas are good or bad. As with anything in life, it is up to you to choose whether it's for you or not. Don't shun an idea because it is New Age and, by the same token, don't automatically agree with it because it claims to be.

But isn't the New Age really the Devil's tool? There are many people who think that the New Age heralds the arrival of the anti-Christ.

This may stem from the fact that some New Age churches which have grown out of older, more traditional Christian churches have embraced ideas from other spiritual paths - ideas such as reincarnation, karma and dharma. Members of Christian churches which have incorporated these principles into their Christianity are no less followers of the teachings of Christ than those who belong to the more traditional sects. In fact, many New Age churches have carefully reviewed the teachings of Jesus and strive to follow his teachings directly rather than following the interpretations which have evolved over the last 2,000 years.

Rather than defend the New Age against this powerful accusation, let's look more closely at the statement: "The New Age is the devil's tool." It is a statement that arises out of the fear of something different, something unknown.

A lot of the changes that are taking place in the New Age are frightening because they challenge what is held most dear and personal: religious beliefs. Belonging to the New Age does not require anyone to change his or her beliefs. It is an inclusive system - not an exclusive one. It asks only that each of us be able to move spiritually in our chosen direction and that, rather than creating more boundaries, we work toward creating unity and wholeness.

Format Notes

1) Words and phrases are alphabetically listed in **bold type**. The definition follows in plain type.

2) Words within the definition in **bold type** mean that that particular word is defined elsewhere under its own heading. This is to minimize repetition of recurring concepts.

3) At the end of a definition there may be a suggested cross reference. For example: see also **healing at a distance**. This cross-referencing is to help you find more information in a specific area of interest.

4) Definitions are listed 1), 2), 3) when a word has more than one distinct meaning.

5) Many words have meanings beyond what is included here. The definitions in this book will be helpful in understanding most New Age books, lectures, magazine articles, conversations and perhaps your neighbor, co-worker, child, sibling or parent.

6) Some words are labeled either "buzzword," "buzzphrase" or "come to mean." Here is a description of those terms:

Buzzword, Buzzphrase - The jargon of the New Age community. Many words listed as such are words used in everyday language but are included in this dictionary because they have taken on or have been given additional special meaning for the New Age.

Come to mean - Over time, the accepted definition of a word changes from its original meaning. This is the nature of language and the New Age has altered its share of words. The phrase "come to mean" indicates that this is a modified and possibly simplistic version of the original definition

Some common words such as "energy," "vibration," "positive" and "negative" will not always be in bold type even though they are defined in the book. Many times these words will be easily understood from their context. They will be placed in boldface only if understanding of the word being defined is dependent upon understanding one of these words.

∞

The dictionary form was chosen for this book for two reasons. First, if you have specific questions about the New Age, these questions are probably triggered by hearing an unfamiliar word. And now you can look up the word in **The New Age A to Z**. The second reason is that one of the best ways to understand a people or a culture is through the study of its language. And so this book presents the language of the New Age. I hope that whether you choose to read through the "A to Z" portion of the book from "a" to "z," or to jump around in the text, that you gain an understanding of and a feeling for the ideas of the New Age and the people in which they live. I wish you good reading.

The New Age

New Age is not a place or thing. It is a time, an evolution.

New Age is not a goal or destination. It's how you get there.

New Age is not you. It is how you perceive yourself.

New Age is not about being healthy or healed. It's about going toward that state.

New Age has no victims. It is comprised of those who choose their life path.

New Age is not one way. It is your way as you live with an open heart connected to your mind as a part of our grand universe.

New Agers are not frivolous. They have vision and work hand in hand with modern science.

New Age never says never, for all things are possible to a willing heart that is also willing to work toward a goal.

New Age does not use words like good and bad, for both are part of the one universe and these polarities are simply alternate paths and our choices.

New Age chooses love, life and health at every opportunity.

∞ **A** ∞

Acknowledge, acknowledgement - The explicit verbal recognition of qualities, viewpoints, hopes and dreams of another or oneself. This recognition is entirely neutral. Praise and criticism are neither offered nor implied. Acknowledgement simply denotes acceptance of the existence of these viewpoints and is an important component in any relationship with another or with oneself. See also **non-judgmental, validation**.

Activate - 1) Assumes that information or a state of mind is accessible at any given moment but that a stimulus or catalyst is necessary to bring this forward into everyday **consciousness**. This stimulus will bring the information forward into current memory; i.e. it will "activate" the information. 2) Activation of **body memory**, to recall or bring forward a dormant memory stored in the physical body. Often recalled by touch during a **bodywork** session. 3) Activate **past life memory** - to bring alive past experiences through hypnosis or other techniques. 4) For individuals who have an **implant**, it can be "activated" or brought into action. This triggering of the implant might possibly be stimulated by **UFO** contact and instruction; or the implant may take action at a time that is predetermined when the implant is put in place. See also **block, subconscious mind**.

Acupressure - A technique similar to **acupuncture**, except that the meridian points are stimulated by pressure from the therapist's hands or fingers rather than by needles. A special pen-like tool may also be applied to the points. See also **acupuncture, alternative therapies, meridian lines, shiatsu.**

Acupuncture - Ancient Chinese method of stimulating the body's natural healing abilities. Very fine needles are placed into the surface of the skin along specific "acupuncture points." These points are areas of concentrated **energy** along the **meridian lines.** These unseen meridians travel the body from head to foot connecting the major glands and organs. The meridians are responsible for distribution of what is described as an electrical "nerve fluid." There is a relationship between the meridians and health. The meridians either flow freely with energy or they have **blocks.** Acupuncture needles are placed at the blocks or congested points in order to relieve the congestion, thus allowing the energy to flow freely. The body can then heal itself more easily.

Acupuncture can also be used in a reverse manner. The acupuncturist might place needles at certain points to block pain. For example, acupuncture has been used during surgery as an anesthetic. It might also be used to help someone quit smoking by blocking the impulse for cigarettes. See also **nadis.**

Aether - Please see **ether.**

Affirmations - A technique for making **positive** changes in your life through repeating positive, uplifting statements. Much of our behavior and many of our attitudes are based on what we have learned from family or from people we look up to, such as teachers. We assume things about ourselves and the world because we have learned them or have been **programmed** to believe these thoughts. All too often we develop attitudes that are counterproductive to our happiness and well-being. Affirmations are a means of reversing these limiting thoughts and freeing ourselves so that we can our reach our full potential.

When we discover **negative** thought patterns and beliefs which may be contributing to unwanted behavior patterns, we can change the thought patterns from negative to positive by repeating the positive thought.

The first thing we have to do is discover the negative pattern. Then we can create a statement which clearly describes the pattern. The statement is then reworded to describe the desired condition. Words like "not," "won't," "can't" and "no" are carefully avoided. Repetition of the positive statement is said to bring a favorable change or **transformation**.

Affirmations do not have to be personalized. There are books with general affirmation suggestions and **subliminal tapes** with affirmations to help you reach your goals. See also **Course in Miracles, mantra, self-hypnosis**.

Age of Aquarius - Also known as the **New Age**. You may be familiar with the phrase "This is the dawning of the age of Aquarius" from the song in the Broadway musical hit "Hair."

Aquarius is one of the twelve signs of the **zodiac**. Astrologers have divided up long periods of time much as they have divided the heavens.

Time has been divided into "ages" and the names of the ages correspond to the names of the signs of the zodiac. As it happens, Moses lived in the age of Aries, Jesus in the age of Pisces. We are now coming out of the age of Pisces and entering into the age of Aquarius. Each age has the characteristics of the zodiacal sign for which it is named. A particularly interesting fact is that while personal astrological signs move in a progression of Aquarius, Pisces, Aries etc., the ages of the planet progress in an opposite motion of Aries, Pisces, Aquarius, etc.

The moment for the change from the age of Pisces to the age of Aquarius is debatable. The dates range from the years 1987 to 2000 to 2010 to 2025. Perhaps these differences have to do with calculations that correspond to different calendars. Given that an age lasts a little more than two thousand years, thirty eight years isn't a large discrepancy. We are close enough to the age of Aquarius to begin to welcome in - you got it - the New Age.

For a clue to the characteristics of the Aquarian Age, one can study the zodiacal sign of Aquarius, "the water bearer." The symbol of Aquarius is that of a man in the sky emptying a pitcher. Presumably, the substance in the pitcher is something of higher cosmic influence and flows onto us mortals below. It is not clear that such a study would help in discovering an accurate picture of what the New Age means in the context of our everyday lives. See also **Harmonic Convergence, Introduction.**

Akashic records - Like a computer file, only made of **ether**. In the akashic records, every person has a file where every thought, emotion and action is recorded. This file is constantly being added to and grows with the person till death and into later **incarnations**. These files are accessible to those who are close to **Spirit**. The records can be read but they cannot be altered. Records are always read in the language of the **reader** or seeker. They are received into the **awareness** of the reader, not "read" like a book. See also **psychic**.

Alchemy - Dates back to ancient Egyptian times. Although we all have a tendency to picture the medieval sorcerer standing over bubbling flasks turning base metals into gold, alchemy, in addition to being a physical process, is a mental and spiritual process of bringing that which is of a lower, denser vibration into a higher, lighter vibration. The alchemist's goal is to be able to change physically, to reach the stage of being able to dematerialize and rematerialize the physical body at will thus achieving immortality. Turning base metals into gold is only the first lesson for the alchemist (one who practices alchemy) and is considered by many to be a metaphor for spiritual refinement. Chemistry was developed as a direct outgrowth of alchemy. See also **transmutation**.

Alexander method - A system of movement exercises which focuses on everyday movement: talking, walking, standing, sitting. The purpose of these exercises is to re-educate the physical body to move easily, to eliminate **stress** and pain caused by incorrect posture and inefficient muscle movement.

ALF - Acronym for "alien life form." See also **alien, EBE, ET**.

Alien - come to mean - Alien life form or extraterrestrial biological entity. A being from another planet. See also **ALF, EBE, ET**.

Alien abduction - There are thousands of reports which tell stories of people who have been relocated from their homes and vehicles to alien space ships. This type of action is described in the popular book *Communion: A True Story* by Whitley Strieber. The reasons for alien abductions are not fully understood but are assumed to be for scientific research by the **ALF**'s. See also **cattle mutilations, government conspiracy, implants, UFOlogy**.

Allopathic medicine - The branch of medicine which treats ailments with agents which produce a dissimilar effect from that of the disease. Generally speaking, medicines are prescribed because they diminish the symptoms of the disease. Although symptoms are relieved or become manageable, this does not necessarily mean that the disease has gone away. This theory of medicine is opposite to **homeopathy**. Allopathy is the theory behind medical treatment as approved by the American Medical Association. See also **alternative therapies, holistic health therapies, homeopathy**.

Altar - The New Age altar is different from the traditional altar in that the individual can choose what the altar looks like and what its function is. Often the altar is small and in a very private location in the home. There may be candles, **crystals**, religious pictures or pictures of loved ones. There may also be objects relating to **healing** or **manifesting**. The New Age altar, like the traditional altar, is used as a point of focus. Sometimes **meditation** is practiced in front of the altar; however, the altar might merely exist in the home as a symbol of devotion. See also **healing at a distance, ritual**.

Alternative realities - See **simultaneous realities**.

Alternative therapies - Accepted umbrella name for healing therapies which are not traditional in our western culture. Keep in mind however, that therapies such as **acupuncture** are fully accepted in the East as primary treatment, not as an alternative or option. Sometimes the word "alternative" is used as a euphemism to describe a therapy which is not an **allopathic** therapy - that is, one accepted by the American Medical Association, the generally accepted standard of treatment in the United States.

American Indian Ceremony and Religion - See **Native American culture**.

Amulet - Usually a natural object such as a sea shell, stone or feather, although it may be an object made for the particular purpose of being an amulet. The amulet is carried or worn as **protection**. It can be protection from any kind of trouble, from disease or evil spirits, or psychic protection. The owner generally designates the specific use for the amulet.

The natural **vibrations** of the object can be enhanced by the owner's thoughts and the object can enhance the psychic powers of the owner. See also **talisman**.

Androgyny - A true androgynous state is one in which a person is structurally and functionally both male and female. As human beings we display the physical characteristics of one sex or the other. However, we all have both male and female characteristics within us. And overseeing all of this, there is a spirit or soul that is neither male nor female. See also **anima-animus, duality, female principle, male principle, yang, yin**.

Angel - The title of a level achieved in the multi-leveled or hierarchical **etheric world intelligence**. This level of achievement is gained over many lifetimes of purifying the spirit or by coming up through the ranks, first as a **nature spirit**. Angels are "messengers" as the Greek root word indicates. Within the rank of angel, there are many levels. The **deva** or nature angel, the guardian angel or **guide, healing masters** and archangels are the ones most spoken about in the New Age. Angels do not have earthly bodies. However, they can lower the vibratory rate of their bodies and make appearances in what look like human bodies. When asked, angels bring help and wisdom to those on earth. The asking may be done consciously or unconsciously. See also **deva, elementals, elf, fairy**.

Anima - animus - These are the names that Carl **Jung** gave to the masculine feelings of assertiveness and power within the female, known as animus and the feminine feelings of softness and compassion within the male, known as anima. See also **androgyny, Jung**.

Ankh - The ankh is of ancient Egyptian origin. Its meaning is "life," "living," "life that cannot die." The ankh is one of the earliest **amulets**. Egyptians were often buried with the ankh and there is reason to believe that they also wore it and used it while they were alive. There are many an-cient Egyptian paintings and sculptures depicting gods and goddesses holding the ankh. It was thought that life was given to mortal beings by the gods through use of the ankh. Scholars are uncertain as to whether the ankh is only a symbol or actually existed.

Aquarian Age - See **Age of Aquarius, New Age**.

Aromatherapy - The treatment of ills by essential oils. Although modern aromatherapy is approximately 400 years old, in its ancient forms it has been practiced all over the world and may be as much as 5000 years old. The oils are extracted from herbs, flowers, roots, seeds, fruits, grasses, tree gums, wood and leaves. Usually the oils are massaged into the skin. In very rare situations, they are taken internally. Some of the benefits of essential oils are: relaxation, mood stimulation and stimulation of the **immune system**. Some oils have been well-documented for their outstanding antiseptic properties. See also **alternative health therapies**.

A.R.E. - Association for Research and Enlightenment. The library in Virginia Beach, Va. devoted to the study and preservation of the transcripts of Edgar Cayce's **readings**. There are branches in other cities across the country. See also **Edgar Cayce**.

Ascendant, or ascending sign, or rising sign - Pertains to **astrology**, the ascendant or rising sign is determined by creating an astrological chart. The ascendant is the constellation which is on the eastern horizon at the moment of birth. For those who are moderately interested in astrology, the ascending sign, the **sun sign** and the **moon sign** are the most important signs to be aware of. Knowing these three signs gives the lay person a better understanding of self or another than does knowing just the **sun sign**. The ascendant illustrates your physical make up and how you project yourself to the world.

Ascended master - One who has reached an advanced state of being, transmuted the earthly body and become one with **Spirit**. Although the Ascended masters do occasionally appear on earth in their physical bodies to teach, usually they teach through others because if they appear in physical form they run the risk of being worshipped. This would be counterproductive at this time when the message is that each of us is a manifestation of Spirit and we do not need to worship Spirit in another. Ascended masters can also be **channeled**. See also **transmutation**.

Ascension - Through the process of purification, most usually developed through **meditation,**

there is a speeding up of the molecular **vibration** of the components of the human system, the spirit, mind and body. The process of Ascension occurs when the vibrations of these components become higher and higher or lighter and lighter - literally enlightened. In becoming lighter, the body will begin to rise from the ground. Complete ascension may also be thought of as moving from the **third dimension** into another, rather than actually going from one place to another.

Ashram - A place similar to a monastery used by the various **Hindu** (native to India) sects. At an ashram, disciples may live removed from the everyday world where they can concentrate on their spiritual lives. They usually work for their room and board in whatever jobs are necessary to the running of the ashram.

An ashram also functions much like a church in that people are free to come and visit the ashram and participate in the spiritual practices although they might not want to dedicate their lives to this way of living. Visitors are often offered instruction in the sect's ways.

There are ashrams scattered around the United States which welcome people and families for short periods of time. This can be a unique opportunity for people to have a "spiritual holiday" instead of traveling or going to a regular vacation resort. See also **retreat**.

Ashtar - Ashtar and the **Ashtar Command** have been known through **channels** for forty years or more. Ashtar has described himself as seven feet tall, with blue eyes. He comes from Venus and is the "Supreme Director in charge of all the spiritual program" for the earth, commanding the Brotherhood of Light - Airborne Division. He is second in command, with only **Sananda** above him.   He is responsible for the earth and is dedicated to universal peace. His mission is one of love.

Ashtar, who resides somewhere in space on his spaceship, maintains that the earth is in danger because of disruptions in its magnetic field.   This has been caused by overwhelming negative emotions which have resulted in murders, wars and nuclear experimentation. Ashtar also warns of great natural disasters which can still be avoided by correcting the patterns of negative actions and thoughts.

Ashtar is bound by the laws of the universe and cannot interfere with any race or planet unless there is a nuclear war, which would also threaten the rest of the universe.   In this case Ashtar would have to somehow stop the war and/or evacuate the planet. This he could easily do, for his spaceship or "mothership" is 100 miles across, and is only one in the fleet of the **Ashtar Command**. See also **earth changes**.

Ashtar Command - As described by **Ashtar** through many **channels** over forty or more years, the Ashtar Command is part of the Confederation of Planets for Peace, which is part of the Federation of Free Worlds, which includes all space commands throughout the universe. The mission of the Ashtar Command is to keep in contact with planet earth and monitor activity on the planet. Its mission is also to communicate with those on earth and warn of possible disasters to the planet. The command includes twenty million extraterrestrial beings who are involved with the program for planet earth and whose aim it is to bring peace to the planet. Additionally, there are approximately four million people on earth who are consciously or unconsciously involved. The Ashtar Command is a relatively local command, only covering our solar system. See also **Ashtar**.

Assist - buzzword. 1) The term often used to describe what a **healer** does when treating another person; for example, a practitioner may have a dialogue with a client and gently guide the client to a sought-after understanding. Also used in **bodywork**. 2) A person may "assist" in a **workshop**. This is done by someone who has already gone through the workshop and would like to attend the workshop again to gain deeper knowledge of the material. Those who assist do not generally participate in the same manner as those taking the workshop. Instead, they may serve as aides to the leader of the workshop and those who attend.

Astral body - The astral body is an exact copy of the physical body. It is made of a finer material and can pass through the material world uninhibited by walls and other physical objects. This body is reported to have a lustrous appearance and is also known as the "body of light" and "light body." The astral body usually stays aligned with the physical body but the astral body has the ability to leave the physical body and travel. See also **astral projection, out of body experience**.

Astral plane, astral level, astral worlds - Includes the physical world and extends beyond it. Reference to the astral plane is usually to that part of the astral world which lies outside the realm of the physical. The etheric world is beyond the astral and it includes both the astral and physical planes. They are all interlocked but distinctions are made among them because of the distinct quality of activity on those planes.

Think of the entire etheric world as a three layer cake. The bottom layer is dense, heavy chocolate (the physical), the second is chocolate swirl pound cake (the astral) and the top layer is the lightest angel food (the etheric).

The astral plane has gotten a bad reputation because it is where the "lower" or less spiritually minded beings reside. This is where ghosts and other mischievous **entities** can be found. Remember that not all beings on the astral are malevolent, just as the physical plane is not all bad even though it is the densest level of existence. You will find that there are varying definitions and divisions of these planes in the teachings of different schools of thought. See also **etheric plane**.

Astral projection - Also known as "out of body experience" (or OBE) and **astral travel**. The experience of someone viewing the world from a point outside of the physical body. These fairly common experiences which are shared by a surprising number of people are divided into two main categories. First, the "parasomatic" experience where a person inhabits and travels in a second body which is an identical double of the physical self and often clothed in a manner identical to that of the physical body. Second is the "asomatic" experience or travel without a body. A person who has had this experience might describe it as "just being," while at the same time having the ability to see and sense. The OBE is almost always characterized by feelings of joy, elation and well-being with no loss of the powers of memory or reasoning.

Many OBE's happen spontaneously and cannot be either predicted or controlled. Some people claim to be able to leave their body "at will." It is possible that by learning special concentration, relaxation and meditation tech- niques, the individual may be able to control the experience. **Yogis, shamans** and **mystics** of other cultures have claimed that they are able to travel the astral plane "at will." Proof of OBE's is that people have visited places and witnessed events while their physical bodies were asleep at home. Through astral travel, they had know- ledge that would otherwise have been impossible to have. Open-minded reading of detailed re- ports of such experiences leaves little or no room for disbelief of the phenomenon. Scientists and philosophers alike are challenged with the reality of the OBE which has, to date, no satis- factory explanation.

Astral travel - Same as **Astral projection**.

Astrocartography - Similar to **astrology**. Using the birth date and time, a chart is developed. The chart shows a world map and contains lines relating to planetary movement. The lines are generated according to birth time information. Astrocartography is based on the idea that your global location is important because as your location on the planet changes, the configuration of planets which influence you also changes. The lines indicating the influences of the planets tell what general type of experiences, opportunities and emotional framework you can expect at a particular location. Some places may prove best for family harmony and others good for career openings. Yet other locations may prove to work against you. Astrocartography can be useful when you are considering a move to another part of the country or world or as a help in understanding your present home more fully. See also **astrology**.

Astrologer, astrologist - One well-versed in **astrology**. Someone who can create an astrological chart and interpret it.

Astrological reading - The process of having an **astrologer** explain the meaning of the chart generated from your birth date, place and time. See **astrology** for more complete information.

Astrology - Described by Webster as " prediction of events by the stars." Being as much an artist as a scientist, the **astrologer** creates an astrological chart or horoscope using the exact date, time and place of birth. In the creation of this chart, mathematics and the astrologer's knowledge of the movement of the planets are used. The exact position of the planets of our solar system are charted at the moment of birth. This information is most commonly arranged by the astrologer in a circle which is divided like a pie into "houses."

heart rate and other body functions generally thought to be automatic. There are several different types of bio-feedback machines but they work in similar ways. The subject is hooked up to a machine (with, for example, small electrodes on the skin). The machine then uses a visual representation, such as a graph or blinking lights, to show or "feed back" information such as heart rate and brain activity. As the thought patterns of the subject vary, output from the machine varies. It is, therefore, possible to see how thoughts and emotions affect the body. The subject then is able, at will, to alter thought patterns and bring about the desired change in the body. Bio-feedback is a **tool** to help better understand the mind-body connection.

Bio-magnet - A magnet used in healing. Generally, a small magnet prepared with an adhesive so that it can be worn on the skin for hours or days at a time. Bio-magnets may also be made into strips or blocks depending on their application. The only difference between a bio-magnet and a regular bar or horseshoe magnet is the shape. The bio-magnet has a larger surface of each magnetic pole exposed for easy application to the body. See also **magnets, healing with**.

Block, blockage - 1) A break in the flow of energy in the auric field, physical body, emotions or **meridian lines**. 2) The word block usually means a physical obstruction and has come to describe a psychological condition. The New Age has expanded the meaning to include any limitations a person may have whether self-generated or brought about by outside influences.

Body memory - Although we usually think of "remembering" as something done only by the mind, the body has its own memory and stores important information. Body memory records experiences in the physical body. This memory might extend to **past lives**. 1) Through **activation** of your body memory, you might recall important information that your mind is unable to remember. Perhaps you were too young or the incident was so painful that the memory has been **blocked** and is not available. Nevertheless, the memory has been recorded in your body. Asking your body may be the most direct way to recover the information. Using the wealth of body memory, it is possible to understand and release psychological difficulties. To do this, both your mind and body must receive attention.

A healer who understands body memory will **release** your body memory to heal your body. If only your mind gets attention, the difficulty will appear again until your body memory is healed or released. 2) It is felt that recurring injuries to or diseases located in a particular part of your body could be related to memories stored in that area of your body and that these injuries and diseases can be healed by working with that part of your body directly. Some therapies which work specifically with releasing unwanted body memory are **Rolfing**, **Hellerwork, polarity therapy and chiropractic**.

Bodywork - buzzword. **Massage** or other physical therapy requiring the practitioner to manipulate the physical body in some way. If therapy is described as a "bodywork session," assume that you will lie on a table of some kind and that the therapist will be touching you. In some types of bodywork the patient remains fully clothed; in other types, the patient will disrobe and be draped with a towel or sheet.

Buddha - 1) One who has been enlightened or awakened to the true nature of existence. 2) Historically, a particular man, Siddhartha Gautama, born about 563 B.C.E. near what is today Nepal. After years of studying with great teachers on his search for spiritual realization, he found liberation of the body and mind; he became **enlightened**. Siddhartha taught for some thirty five years until his death.

Known as "the" Buddha, Siddhartha Gautama is not worshipped as a god or savior but is revered and adored as a human being who sought and found human perfection. He is considered by many to be an **avatar**, one of many who came to earth to teach as predicted by the Vedas, the **Hindu** book of knowledge.

The Buddha and his teachings, which are called **dharma**, teach "the middle way" and have become the focal point for **Buddhism**.

Buddhism, buddhist - The traditions of Buddhism have a history of 2500 years. However, the word "Buddhism" was coined, quite surprisingly, only about 300 years ago. Buddhism includes the many different religious sects found in countries such as Sri Lanka, Burma, Thailand, China, Tibet, Korea and Japan. The sects all have in common the teachings and values of the **Buddha**. Other commonalties among Buddhist sects are, according to religious scholars: a) the establishment of monasteries; b) the idea of non-self (anatman), the part of a being that is not personality, feelings, desires or mind; c) the idea of emptiness or the void (sunyata) as the Supreme Reality; and d) the goal of reaching nirvana or the realization of absolute reality, where liberation from the cycle of birth, death and rebirth is found. To become liberated in this way is the ultimate goal for the **Buddhist**.

For the Buddhist, the goal of nirvana is to merge with the void realizing that each person is God - every person, all on earth, is God. This idea is well-accepted by the New Age and has crept into some New Age offshoots of the Christian religions. Less understood by many is the concept of non-self (anatman) or the idea that there is no fixed self which lasts into the next incarnation, but that a person is a sequence of events (**karma**), feelings, perceptions and desires. What is **reincarnated** is not what we know as personality; rather it is the result of the actions of the personality. See also **Zen**.

∞ C ∞

Call in - buzzphrase. 1) When you want to have a dialogue with one of your **spirit guides** or **spirit teachers** or any other **spirit beings**, you can contact them by "calling them in." This is done by asking them, either silently or aloud, to be available to you for a conversation. 2) When you want to have a particular non-spirit **energy** available, such as **protection** or peace, you can invoke it using this method.

Candles, candle magic - Candles are burned on an **altar** in many religions and so it is on the New Age altar. Different colored candles may be used. This use of colored candles has its roots in **pagan** religions. In addition, today we associate the different colors with different **chakras**.

Those involved in the **pagan** or **neo-pagan** religions may use candles in elaborate rituals but the general approach in the New Age is much simpler. Candles can be burned to give a particular atmosphere to a room. A prayer or wish can be expressed and then a candle lit and left to burn as a constant expression of this prayer. Each of the colored candles has a different meaning. White is for purity and highest spiritual intent. Violet, for increased spirituality and guidance. Blue is lit for peace, healing, tranquility and increased communication among individuals. Pink, for love and happiness. Green, for prosperity in health and fortune. Yellow or orange, for greater understanding and inner strength.

Cattle mutilations - There is much documen-
tation on the thousands of cattle mutilations in
the midwestern and western United States.
Incidents have also been reported in South Africa
and Sweden. Generally, the reproductive organs
are removed in a surgically precise manner. The
groups most concerned, aside from the ranchers,
are the UFOlogists, those who study **UFO's**.
Upon inspection of the bizarre facts, it seems
that the most probable answer to these mysterious mutilations is that they are performed by
alien beings for reasons that are still unclear.
See also **government conspiracy**.

Cayce, Edgar - (1877 - 1945). Cayce, a world
renowned **clairvoyant**, is known as the "sleeping
prophet." He got this nickname because he
would lie down, go into a **trance**, do his **reading**
from this "asleep" state and when he awoke he
had no recall of what happened during the
reading. He is America's most authenticated
psychic. Many of the 14,000 readings he gave
over a period of 43 years dealt with health problems of individuals. Medical doctors would often
come to him when they were stumped by a case.
Cayce would uncover the root of the patient's
problem and recommend a treatment plan.
    When doing a reading for someone not
present, Cayce only needed the name and address of the person to tune in and get the information in question. Cayce used his clairvoyant
talents to make global as well as personal predictions. While in the clairvoyant state, he also
expounded on many subjects including **Atlantis**,
ESP, dreams, **reincarnation** and science. The
transcripts from Cayce's readings are preserved

in Virginia at the **A.R.E.** (The Association for Research and Enlightenment, Inc.) and are available for study at the library in Virginia Beach. Some of this tremendous volume of information has been published recently in edited versions. Also, some of the more common remedies that Cayce recommended over the years are specially prepared to his specifications and are available commercially. See also **akashic records, hook into.**

Cell memory - Refers to behavior patterns and thought patterns for which there is apparently no first hand experience, no discernible reason for the memory. This type of memory might not be stored in the conventionally recognized area for memory - the brain - but in other cells throughout the body. Scientifically, this is referred to as genetic encoding. It is believed that this stored information can affect the personality, behavior and emotions as well as the physical body. It is different from **body memory** in that it has nothing to do with individual personal experience but is passed on from one's ancestors. See also **body memory.**

Center - 1) Your axis or core. The solar plexus area or third **chakra** and what it represents. Your point of **personal power**. Some feel that the center is located closer to the second chakra, the place of personal creativity. 2) "Find my center" or "to center myself" - buzzphrases. Meaning, find my balance in any moment or any situation. 3) Speaks of the spiritual and architectural balance point of the body. 4) An organization or meeting place.

Ceremony - Ceremony and **ritual** have their roots in time immemorial and their place in religions all around the world. Their enactment includes the use of incense, special clothing and, perhaps, special food and drink. The New Age ceremony, like the New Age **altar**, can take many forms and draw from many traditions. The reasons for ceremony have changed little through time. The usual reason for ceremony is to invoke a particular state of mind in the participants so that they can go beyond the rational and toward a more **mystical experience**. See also **ritual**.

Chakra, cakra, chakra system - Sanskrit, literally "circle" - more often translated as "wheel." The chakra system has roots that can be traced back thousands of years to the **Hindu** tradition. The chakra system consists of seven centers which run along the vertical midline of the body and relate to the important glands and organs of the body. Because they are concentrations of subtle energy, they are invisible to the untrained eye. They have been described as spinning vortexes or whirlpools of colored light but this description misses the three dimensional quality of the chakras.

　　The function of the chakra is to bring subtle energy into the body, thus nourishing the body. The chakras also radiate energy outward from the body and this outward radiation of energy can be an indicator of the health of that particular area of the body. Understand also, that in this tradition, different areas of the body correspond to different functions that we in the West attribute to personality and intellect and locate in the mind or brain. Each chakra has a name, a function for the physical body and the spirit as well as a color, a sound and a corresponding shape. In the West, the naming of the chakras has been somewhat simplified by using a number and a short English phrase in place of the unfamiliar Sanskrit names.

They are numbered from bottom to top along the spine: 1st chakra - the root or base of the spine, the color is black to deep red. 2nd chakra - the navel, creative or sexual chakra, bright red to orange. 3rd chakra - the solar plexus or stomach chakra, orange to yellow. 4th chakra - the heart area and the bridge between the lower/physical and upper/spiritual, pink or its color complement, green. 5th chakra - the base of the throat and the communication/will chakra, blue. 6th chakra - the brow or third eye, indigo or violet. 7th chakra - the crown or the gateway to **Spirit**, violet or white.

The chakras color the **aura**. When someone is in a state of health, the chakras will glow or radiate in equal intensity with a pure, light color. In a state of illness, they might be seen as out of balance. When a chakra is not functioning properly it will have a color which is grayed or darkened and all the chakras might not glow with equal intensity. See also **aura**.

Channel - 1) Noun, one who channels. A channel is one who allows his or her consciousness to be used by another intelligent **spirit** source. The spirits which "come through" are many and diverse in type. Some channels go into an altered state or **trance** when they are used. Others are fully conscious.

The conscious channel seems to hear or sense the **entity** internally and immediately relays the information to whomever is present or records it in another way, such as on a tape recorder or by writing it down. Channeled entities are usually beings who were once on earth. However, they might also be **spirit beings** or angels of any level in the hierarchy. Occasionally, it has happened that someone currently on the planet in a distant location is channeled. The archangel **Michael** comes through quite frequently, as do **Sananda** and **Ashtar**. Some channels bring forth information from their own **higher self**.

Little is really known about this phenomenon and how it occurs. It is recommended that the information given be assessed for the value that it brings in and of itself rather than because it is channeled.

2) Verb, to channel. What happens when people allow an **entity** to speak through them. See also **channeled information**.

Channeled information - This may be information about past, present or future and may be on any topic. The information may be oral or transcribed in book form. The information may even be revealed through **automatic writing**. It may be "new" in that it has not been previously made public or it may be previously related material that is explained differently. The information "comes through" a **channel**. The source of the information can be discarnate **entities**, **elementals**, **angels**, archangels, **ET's**, **light beings**, those who have left the earth or the channel's own **higher self**.

Channeling session - A time period set aside for one or more people to channel. The session can be private, addressing the specific needs of an individual, as in a **reading**, or can be offered to the general public and perhaps touch on social and global issues. One or more people might **channel** at a session and a single individual may channel single or multiple **entities**.

Chanting - The repetition of a sound, word or words in a constant rhythm and a simple melody for a particular purpose. Throughout religious history, chanting has been one of the highest spiritual rituals. See also **mantra, toning**.

Charge, emotional charge - A memory which has a particularly strong sensation attached to it is said to have an emotional charge. When this memory is accessed - perhaps not consciously - or a situation similar to the one which caused the memory occurs, one might respond with an emotion seemingly inappropriate to the situation because of the emotional charge. What causes a memory to have such an emotional charge is very individual in nature.

Charge, energize - To direct one's focus into an object with such strong feeling or thought that the object takes on the same feeling or thought. The object cannot actually think or feel the thought. Rather, it holds the feeling or thought as an unseen **vibration** or energy pattern. Those who are able to sense these vibrations or energy patterns and interpret them can put the feeling or thought back into words. This "object reading" is known as psychometry.

Ch'i - Chinese. The universal "breath" that resides in all things and people. Life force or energy. A synonym for ch'i is **prana**. See **prana** for a more in depth definition.

Child within, inner child - This is the young person inside each and every one of us. Also known as the real self, the child within is the fun loving, inquisitive, loving being unspoiled by social pressures and demands.

Chiropractic - The theory and practice of manipulating the bones of the body, mainly the spine, in order to place them into a more perfect alignment. Particularly helpful after an accident or injury. Also quite effective in treating a weakness which may have been present from birth. Chiropractic focuses on relieving discomfort caused by any misalignment of the body.

Chiropractor - One who has trained in the science of **chiropractic** and who practices this science. Chiropractors must be licensed to practice just as medical doctors are.

Clairaudience - The **psychic** ability to hear sounds in the form of music or words when there is no one present to make those sounds. Although the sounds seem to come from somewhere outside the consciousness of the hearer, someone standing nearby will not be able to hear them. Sometimes however, the sounds seem to be happening inside the hearer's head.

Clairvoyance - The **psychic** ability to receive images and information from the non-physical world. These images are seen inside the head with the seer's inner vision. Sometimes these images come in the form of pictures, individual to the psychic receiving the pictures. It is up to the psychic to interpret the picture.

Cleansing, clearing - A purification. Cleaning up any thing or person on the physical, astral or etheric levels. To clean the **aura** of an object or person. Depending on the situation, there are a number of different ways to accomplish this purification. See also **light, smudge**.

Co-create - The concept that we as human beings create our world with Spirit or God. Spirit, the highest, purest being, works through us. However, we also have the ability to choose our actions and thoughts and thus alter the world around us. See also **co-evolution, free will**.

Co-dependency - The name for a network of relationships which evolve around people with various addictions (drugs, alcohol, work) and their families. Each addicted person is seen in the larger context of the family or social group. When one person suffers from an addiction, it can usually be seen that he or she is supported in the addiction by the group in one way or another. Each person in the family group is affected by the addictive person and it can be seen that each member of the group is, in some way, also addicted to the difficult situation. See also **holism**.

Co-evolution - The manner in which humans, animals and the planet itself evolve in relation-

ship to each other. Each time one species makes
a change in its habits or has a change made to it
from an outside force, other species must change
also. The domino effect is apparent here. The
earth and its inhabitants are interdependent.
See also **co-create, holism**.

Collective consciousness -   The totality of
thoughts, feelings, sensations and knowledge of
humanity throughout all time. Collective consciousness can be experienced by the individual
in dreams or in "knowing" something not ever
consciously learned. This collective consciousness can be tapped directly by a **channel**. Although it appears that there are some constants
in the collective consciousness, it is always
changing and being added to by our personal
thoughts, feelings and sensations. Its effect on
the earth is difficult to assess.

Colonic - A therapy which promises health
benefits through periodic flushing of the colon.
Similar to an enema but more thorough. Usually
given in a series by a trained practioner and
recommended for specific and serious disease.

Color therapy - Color is used in the form of
colored light bulbs, or white light projected
through colored gels. The colors are projected
onto the body or fed to the body through the
eyes. It is thought that deficiencies in certain
color rays in the body will result in disease.
Either a particular body requires larger doses of
certain colors naturally, or it may be deficient in
certain colors simply because of lack of exposure
to them. Such a deficiency can occur when there

is a lack of natural sunlight. It can also occur when a lot of time is spent in an area that has an abundance of a particular color and a lack of another. Color therapy is considered one of the **vibrational healing** therapies. See also **full spectrum lighting**.

Connection to . . . - buzzphrase. Used in the context of "I feel a connection to my Aunt" or any particular person, place or object. The connection is not physical. It seems to arise from some non-physical reality and its presence shows that someone or something has touched your deep emotions. This feeling of being connected usually occurs forcefully and immediately, without the benefit of a long association. Often there is a sense that some sort of **past life connection** exists. See also **cosmic connection**.

Conscious dreaming - See also **Eckankar, lucid dreaming**.

Consciousness - 1) The totality of what a person thinks, feels, senses and does throughout life. 2) The unseen, forever moving energy of the Universe. 3) Can be used as a term for **Spirit** or God. 4) Any particular level of understanding. If seen in a scale or spectrum, anywhere from no **awareness** whatsoever to **enlightenment**.

"Conscious (any verb)ing" - buzzword. Used in the context of "conscious parenting," "conscious gardening" or "conscious cooking." This phrase indicates that whatever activity is being done, is done with a great deal of thought and care. See also **awareness, unconscious**.

Contract - Also known as life plan. It is thought that before birth, a dialogue takes place between the soul wishing to **incarnate** and those of the **spirit world** who no longer need to incarnate. The purpose of this dialogue is to set up the soul's framework of experience on the **earth plane**. Parents are chosen. The sex of the body that the soul is to inhabit is agreed upon. And the **lessons** that are to be focused on in that lifetime are decided upon. See also **astrology, numerology**.

Cosmic connection - An unusually timely meeting or understanding with another human or object. See also **connection to . . ., past life connection**.

Cosmic consciousness - 1) State of awareness of one's connection to all that comprises the universe. 2) The highest spiritual truths.

Course in Miracles - This is truly a course - a teaching - on our approach to life. It is a unique blending of eastern thought, psychology and Christianity. Although the course uses language which sounds as if it is oriented to the Christian belief system, it is non-sectarian.

The aim of the *Course in Miracles* is to heal our personal conflicts, thus bringing **inner peace**. And only when we each one find inner peace, will the way be open for us to achieve peace outside in the world.

The course has interesting origins in that it was transcribed by Helen Schucman and Bill Thetford from an inner voice heard by Helen. The transcriptions were completed in 1972.

Create - Through desire or action you can bring a particular opportunity or situation into your life. You can do this knowingly through **affirmation** and prayer, or unknowingly through deep, unacknowledged desires and fears. Award for phrase most often heard goes to: "You create your own reality." See also **manifest**.

"Cruelty free" - A claim on labels of various cosmetics and household cleaners. It is meant to indicate that no animal products have been used and no testing has been done on animals during the research and development of the product. However, this type of labeling has no legal meaning and is a marketing tool only.

    The Cosmetics, Toiletries and Fragrances Association does not support this form of labeling because it is unfair to companies who do pioneering research. It is also unfair to the consumer in that it is misleading information.

Crystals - Although crystals are often used to symbolize the New Age, they have no particular meaning in and of themselves - they simply are. The question "what does a crystal mean?" is like pointing to a hair dryer and asking "what does it mean?" It has no meaning as such. It has a func-  tion. It is a **tool**. 1) A crystal is the purest expression of the mineral kingdom. 2) "Crystal" usually pertains to quartz crystal, one mineral among many to form crystals. Can be used for amplification of thought, for healing or in meditation. 3) Used as a connection to other planes of existence such as the etheric (perhaps in **channeling**). Crystals and other minerals have been used throughout history as points of focus in healing and other spiritual **rituals**. They have enjoyed a renaissance of enormous proportions recently. 4) The term **crystal** might be used to mean any gemstone or mineral used for **healing**, although this is technically incorrect since not all gemstones form crystals. See also **channeling, crystal healing, vibrational healing**.

Crystal essences - Please see **gem elixirs**.

Crystal healing - A therapeutic session using crystals as the conduit for **healing energy**. The energy comes either directly from the crystal, from the **healer** who is holding the crystal or is brought from the outside, through the healer and the crystal. Each type of crystal is used much like a prescription for a particular drug is used - for its own properties and effects on the human system. These properties and effects have to do with the **vibration** of the crystal and how it emits energy within its own particular range of vibration or frequency. The effect of crystals in the human system is primarily on the **aura**, cleansing it, clearing up **blocks** and bringing the **subtle bodies** of the aura into harmony and balance. See also **aura, chakras, crystal wand, crystals, vibration, vibrational healing**.

Crystal wand - 1) Literally, a wand, much like the wands found in fairy tales. There is a framework, usually of metal or wood, which acts as a support for the crystal(s). 2) A **tool** used in **crystal healing** or as a display item.

∞ **D** ∞

Denial - buzzword. 1) Refusal to acknowledge as true something in your life or something about yourself that is troublesome to you or those around you. Whatever this is, it is usually obvious to others though you yourself may not see it. 2) The moment of denial of our true heritage caused a split between **Spirit** and humanity. In refusing to see that we are all God, we have created a gap between Spirit and humanity that has led us to experience life as we know it. See also **Bach, duality, separation**.

Destiny - In general, New Agers do not believe that the future is "written in stone" or predetermined. Part of the New Age belief structure is that life will present us with possibilities and that the choices we make with our **free will** determine our future. In other words, there are many possible futures.

However, the word destiny is frequently used in the context of "perfect destiny." In this case "destiny" is a state of being, come to by making the best possible choice at all times.

Deva - 1) As described in the **Hindu** tradition, devas run the spectrum of divine beings, good and evil. 2) Devas are what many **nature spirits** are called. These are the **spirits** or **energy** forms who help to create, caretake and perpetuate the earth. 3) Deva also describes a woman who embodies the qualities of the **Goddess**. See also **elementals**.

Dharma - Sanskrit. 1) That which sets the universe in motion, keeps it in harmony, preserves it and destroys or absorbs it, theoretically to begin again. 2) The name for the teachings of the **Buddha**. He taught "the middle way," the path between "vulgar pleasure seeking" known as hedonism and "futile self-denial" known as asceticism. Personal dharma determines what is right conduct for the individual. This right conduct is to be determined for oneself at any particular moment and is determined by one's individual search for wholeness. Within the concept of dharma, "sins" are only obstacles that one puts in one's own way; not disobedience or ingratitude to God. Since **Buddhism** is a nondualistic religion, there is no recognition of a separation from God. It follows that conduct of an individual can be considered "good" if it is "correct" for the individual.

Dimensions - A dimension is a way of measuring things. The first dimension can be thought of as a point extending itself into a line. The second dimension can be thought of as a line extending itself into a plane. The third dimension can be thought of as a plane extending itself into a cube, a figure with height, width and depth. The fourth dimension is that of time/space. Try to imagine a cube extending itself into another dimension. Different systems of thought postulate different numbers of dimensions - as few as four and as many as fifteen dimensions have been described.

Disinformation - The term given to untruths which are deliberately set forward as fact, usually by those in authority. This incorrect information is often mixed with truth and therefore it becomes difficult to sift the truth from the lies. Disinformation is given in hopes that the real and true information remains undiscovered. See also **government conspiracy**.

Dolphins - This highly intelligent mammal has been the subject of study for the last thirty or so years. Science has uncovered the fact that dolphins communicate with each other in a sophisticated language not yet understood by humans. These studies have also shown that the dolphin is a very outgoing and friendly mammal. We understand so little about the vast oceans which are home to the dolphin. What does seem clear is that the dolphin has inhabited the waters of earth for a very long time and is beginning to get respect as another intelligent life form with which we co-exist.

There are some who have taken the plight of the dolphin to heart and are seeing to it that they are getting some protection from fishermen who kill them in pursuit of other fish.

Dolphins are so gentle that over the last few years many people have chosen to swim with them. They have come away from the experience feeling that dolphins have much to offer us when we are ready to take the time to listen to them with our hearts. There are some who think that the spirit of the dolphin is from another planet and that the dolphin has an important message for us on earth. See also **whales**.

Double terminated (relates to **crystals**) - A crystal (generally quartz) with two points. The pathway of energy through a double terminated crystal functions like traffic on a two way street. In a crystal with only one point, energy flows in one direction, toward and out the point. In a double terminated crystal, energy flows in both directions. It can act as a bridge between two areas of the body during a **crystal healing**.

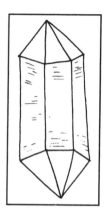

Dowsing - The use of an object such as a **pendulum**, metal rod or forked stick to find something that is hidden from view. Dowsing might be used to lead one to underground water, buried treasure or lost objects. Sometimes used in archaeology for locating ruins and in medicine to find the source of an illness.

Drawn to - buzzphrase. A phrase used when you are attracted to something or someone and this attraction is mystical or unexplained.

Duality - 1) The nature of our physical world and our usual reality where everything seems to have its opposite. **Positive** and **negative, male** and **female**, yes and no, etc. 2) The nature of our relationship to **Spirit**. Spirit above and us as human beings, separate and below. See also **denial, separation**.

∞ **E** ∞

Earth changes - buzzword. Dramatic changes which will alter the earth and the course of human life drastically. Earthquakes, tidal waves, a pole shift, a meteor striking the earth, the sinking of entire land masses and major flooding have all been postulated as possible types of changes based on readings of many religious texts as well as by **psychic** predictions. Many feel that these natural disasters are upon us now and will worsen to peak activity around the years 2000 to 2030. Some think that these changes can be diverted or minimized by the activity of our thoughts. Because the future is constantly being changed by what happens in the present, it is thought that the **free will** of humanity can affect the future of earth.

Earth plane - The three dimensional world. Our physical world on the earth.

EBE's - Pronounced ee-bees, an acronym for extraterrestrial biological entities. See also **ALF**, **alien, ET.**

Eckankar - A modern spiritual path, arising from ancient origins. Introduced to the world by Paul Twitchell during the mid-sixties. Eckankar's goal is freedom through the direct spiritual experience of ECK. ECK is the Holy Spirit which connects the practitioner with the Heart of God, as described in the Eckankar teachings. This connection is accomplished through daily practice of spiritual exercises. These exercises help the Eckist develop an ability for Soul Travel in the dream state.

Additionally, there is an exercise in which the Eckist sings an ancient name of God. Various exercises bring the practitioner into contact with the Holy Spirit or ECK as God's light and sound. Eckankar teaches that we are all spiritual beings and that this knowledge can be awakened through the light and sound of God, bringing divine love into one's life. This is a direct experience of God, awakening the spiritual potential within as it brings increased harmony and understanding into one's life. See also **astral travel, lucid dreaming**.

Ego - A person's personality, belief system, a combination of the **conscious** mind and the **subconscious** mind. Come to mean - A person's undesirable personality traits: anger, greed, jealousy, need for excessive acclaim. "He did it out of ego;" "that's just his ego talking."

Elementals - Unseen by most, these spirit creatures are considered to be the custodians of the earth, those who sustain and perpetuate the four elements. They are described as the fire spirit or Salamander; the air spirit or Sylph; the water spirit or Undine; and the earth spirit or Gnome. The individual names for these **nature spirits**, as they are also called, vary according to different cultures and geographical locations. See also **deva, elf**.

ELF - Acronym for extra low frequency, also known as VLF, for very low frequency. The electromagnetic radiation from high power lines, computer terminals. All cathode ray tubes (including fluorescent lighting and television) and household appliances such as electric blankets and hair dryers emit these low frequency waves. A number of books discuss the hazards to our health and well-being as a result of being exposed to these waves for long periods of time. Although these waves are neither seen nor felt, medical investigation seems to be finding a connection between exposure to ELF waves and **immune system** disorders, cancer, leukemia and a host of other problems. It seems that this information has been ignored and suppressed by utility companies, the electronics industry and the federal government.

Elf, elves - 1) "The little people." Elves have been described by those who see them in many different costumes - wearing little green outfits and caps is one way these **elementals** appear. There are many elf legends, primarily from Europe, which describe elves as being either helpful and playful or as evil, bitter, grumbling little fellows. Elves belong to the earth group of elementals but are sometimes described as **fairies** or the air group. It is possible that these nature spirits have the ability to change form. 2) A person who is of an earthy nature, who can be delightfully and harmlessly mischievous, might be called an elf.

Empowerment - Please see **personal power**.

Energy - Described scientifically as the ability to do work. Energy is observable as motion. For example, air in motion can be a hurricane or a breeze. A breeze has less energy than a hurricane. Energy is observable and measurable and yet, at the same time, is intangible. There are many scientific observations about and characteristics of energy which help us understand things we experience but do not see.

Physics, the science of physical phenomena, studies unseen things such as sounds, vibrations and atoms. (At times, these studies bring the worlds of the scientist and the **metaphysician** very, very close.) Physicists know that energy can be "at work," moving or kinetic energy, such as a running stream. It can be "potential energy" as when a stream is dammed. Energy can be stored. For example, the energy in wood is released when it is burned.

One important tenet in the philosophy of the New Age has been formulated by scientists and is called the "law of conservation." This means that energy can be neither created nor destroyed. However, its form can be changed. Energy is what we call the unseen, intangible, yet measurable force that gives life.

As a buzzword - Anything can have "an energy:" a thought, an object, a person. This intangible "energy" is what emits the qualities we associate with that thought, object or person. "Mark has a very kind energy." "The energy of this room is good." In this context, energy and **vibration** can be used interchangeably. See also **ch'i, prana, reincarnation, vibration.**

Energies, energy (pertaining to a being) - buzzword. A spirit being of any kind which has no physical form. Since these beings do not have visible bodies, they can be considered and are experienced as **vibrations** at a particular rate or frequency. They are referred to simply as energies. This is a way of communicating about unseen intelligences without having to give them human qualities which can be misleading since they are not human.

Enlightened being - One who has found **enlightenment** and serves as an inspiration to others.

Enlightenment - 1) In eastern religions, an inexplicable state of being, designating an experience of oneness with the creator and all creation. The mystery of existence of oneself and all of life is unveiled to the one who attains this, the highest spiritual state of being. 2) Enlightenment has come to mean many different spiritual and intellectual experiences: deep understanding of the connectedness of living creatures; deep sympathy for a person, a situation or an idea; or, perhaps, a feeling of bliss which may happen as a result of meditation or an experience in nature.

All of these experiences, as well as others not mentioned, create an immediate change in the attitude of the one who has had the "enlightening" experience. When the essence of these experiences is brought into daily life, the person who had the experiences may sense more **inner peace**, a greater inner strength and an indefinable feeling of being complete. 3) A view of the world that is peaceful, harmonious and concerned with the well-being of all creatures rather than any one individual, even if that one individual is oneself.

Enneagram - 1) A universal symbol. G.I. Gurd-jieff, master of philosophical psychology and teacher (1872-1949), claimed to have rediscovered this symbol from an ancient source. It is said that all knowledge is included in such a symbol for one who is able to read it. 2) Popular today, the enneagram has inspired the development of a system of nine 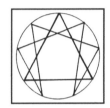 personality types through which we can better understand ourselves, others and our relationships with others.

Entity - come to mean - Any being without a physical body. Synonym for **spirit being, spirit, energy.** See **spirit world beings.**

Environmentalist - A person who is very concerned about, dedicated to and ready to work for the improvement of the condition of the earth. Pollution, landfills, nuclear waste and rain forest defoliation are just a few of the items of concern. Recycling glass, aluminum and paper and using solar energy are some positive measures an environmentalist might take. An environmentalist might make his or her career work positively for the earth or devote volunteer time to one of the numerous organizations whose purpose is to clean up our planet.

Esoteric - Pertains to anything not provable using a scientific methodology or not having a written history - something that is explained by the mysteries of religion, by **psychics** or by other intuitive methods.

ESP - come to mean - To know what will happen in the future. The acronym for extra sensory perception.

ET - Abbreviation for extraterrestrial. Refers to anything not of this earth. Come to mean - A being from another planet. See also **ALF, alien, EBE**.

Ether - Also spelled aether. 1) An indefinable substance that is believed to support the earth and all its inhabitants. An immeasurably fine substance that permeates every atom. 2) That which makes up the **etheric plane**. 3) The ethers or the etheric may refer to anything heavenly, celestial or unseen. Not to be confused with ether, a light, flammable gas used as an anesthetic. See also **chi, prana**.

Etheric body - Although **ether** is part of the physical body, the etheric body refers to that part of a person's unseen energy field which is just outside the physical body. Sometimes the etheric body is said to be inclusive of the **aura** and to extend beyond the aura. Various schools of thought define the etheric body differently.

Etheric double - Another name for the **aura**.

Etheric lines - These lines are used to send thoughts to other people or to help locate information in the **akashic records**. Their purpose is to establish a connection, like the cord used in a tin can "telephone." These lines can be created in your imagination when you need them and are considered to be real on the **etheric**

plane. They are usually generated from the hands or from the top of the head.

Etheric plane - The etheric plane is made of **ether** (not to be confused with the gas used as an anesthetic) and extends infinitely into space. The etheric plane is what could be considered heaven 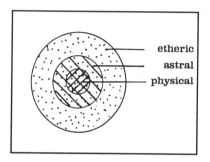 and is the place of highest spiritual values. Technically, the etheric plane includes the **astral plane** and physical plane, but the astral and physical planes are only a portion of the etheric plane and are not purely etheric.

    The physical plane, the world in which we live, is made of the densest matter. It has weight and mass. Beyond the physical (in space) is the astral. Astral matter is finer than physical matter and with training can be seen. It can be sensed by touch and includes the mental and emotional planes as well as the lesser evolved discarnate **entities**. The etheric is finer yet and includes all of the "higher" **energies**. All three planes are interwoven. See also **astral plane, aura, spirit world beings**.

Etheric world intelligence - Etheric world intelligence is part of the world of spirit beings. It exists at the higher levels of beings or intelligences in the etheric world. Some etheric world intelligence **entities** can still **incarnate** on the earth plane and others have evolved beyond the need for incarnating.

This need is based on the idea that earth is a place of learning, a schoolhouse. Once the **lessons** that an intelligence can learn on earth have been completed, there is no need to return. Such a being may choose to incarnate or appear briefly on earth to fulfill an important task, as does an **avatar**. Other more recognizable names given to etheric world intelligences are: deities, invisible intelligence, muse, sylph, unseen force, **angel**, archangel.

Evolution, evolutionary - 1) In the language of the New Age, this is probably the single most used word. Evolution is the ongoing unfolding of the original seed or the continuing of **vibration** after the original vibration. Evolution began the first moment that the universe began. Evolution is a never ending movement toward perfection. Its direction is an upward spiral through successive levels of purity. Evolution is an inevitable natural process. 2) Any change can be seen as a part of an evolution. Destruction itself is a part of this process in the sense that it is a clearing away of the old to make way for the new. See also **co-create, co-evolution, holism**.

Exit, exit the planet - buzzword. To die and therefore leave the **earth plane**. This word implies a continuation of life in some form somewhere else. Also known as a **transition**.

Experience, "to experience the . . ." - buzzword. "Experience" is used rather than hear, see or touch. Describes taking in an event or moment with all the senses. It is probably an expression left over from the "experiences" of the sixties.

Facilitate - buzzword. To make easy. To introduce an object, technique or therapy (a **tool**) which will help the search for health and well-being flow more easily.

Facilitator - 1) One who makes it easier for another to make life changes - may apply to a therapist or **healer**. 2) One who makes it easier for groups to work together. See also **assist**.

Fairy, faerie - One of the elemental spirit beings pictured as delicate, human-like creatures with wings. They are spirits of the air but also may oversee all four elements. See also **deva, elementals, elf**.

Feldenkreis Method - A bodywork method based on the belief that there is a direct relationship between the way we move and the way we feel, think and learn. By gently moving parts of the body in a particular sequence, the Feldenkreis practitioner encourages recipients of the work to explore the images they have of their bodies and their habitual movement patterns. This is done to discover how the entire self is involved in all movement. As awareness increases, functional changes occur, unlocking the untapped potential of the nervous system, expanding mental and physical capabilities.

Female, female energy, feminine principle - Throughout time, the world has been polarized into numerous dualities, one of which is that of the female and the male. The feminine principle is one pole, one aspect, of this duality. The feminine principle exists within all of us - men as well as women. It expresses the nurturing, intuitive, introspective, lunar qualities of our being. It is reflective of rather than a source of light, receptive, cooperative and fertile. It is the ground of being without which the spark of being would simply die. See also **anima-animus, yin, yin-yang symbol**.

Feng-shui - Chinese. The ancient art of placement concerned with the best (most fortuitous) place for dwellings and other architecture. Feng-shui is a geomantic art.

The feng-shui master senses the character of a place by looking at its land formations and determines whether the place is beneficial for living or working. The master's first concern is determining the natural flow, the **ch'i,** the energy of the land, or the ch'i of an existing structure. It is thought that everything has ch'i: buildings, trees, water (above ground and underground), sunlight, etc. People also have ch'i and there is an interaction between the land ch'i and human ch'i affecting the balance of ch'i in people and altering their health and luck in many ways. Building incorrectly, even on very good land, can create a disharmonious situation and have disastrous effects on the lives of those living there. The feng-shui master can determine the things which are disturbing or helpful, down to the smallest detail of decoration.

In cases where the ch'i of a place has been found to be destructive to health or fortune, a feng-shui master can make suggestions to correct this to some degree. It might mean simply rearranging furniture or placing mirrors around a home or office. Although feng-shui comes to many of the same conclusions as science, "good sense" and good design, it is still a mysterious art which often seems illogical. The art of feng-shui is taken quite seriously in China. Still today, especially in the smaller villages where more of the old traditions are maintained, there are masters of feng-shui available for consultation. See also **geomancy, sacred geometry.**

Findhorn Foundation - A spiritual community located in northeast Scotland, Findhorn was founded in 1962 by Peter and Eileen Caddy. The group has managed and turned very poor and barren soil into a farm which supports the Findhorn community. They were able to accomplish this by working closely with nature and the **nature spirits** of the land. "Elixir," a **spirit being**, gave step by step guidance to Eileen Caddy on how to proceed with the project. More than just a garden, the Findhorn community seeks to live in harmony, to demonstrate harmony with each other and with nature. Findhorn is not a **retreat** to get away from the world, it is a place for people to exercise their creativity in building a community which gives form to the reunification of the physical and spiritual aspects of life.

Flotation tank, flotation therapy - A tank filled with a dense epsom salts solution. It is a closed environment, free from external noise and other distractions. As the user of the tank floats like a cork in the mineral solution, pressure, tension and pain are released from all the muscles, the back and the joints. Flotation is said to increase **right-brain** activity, thus bringing on a state of heightened creativity or a meditative state. It is very beneficial to listen to a **subliminal tape** during a flotation session. In this quiet, meditative atmosphere, the effects of the tape are multiplied so that the flotation tank becomes a good environment in which to accelerate learning and to experience relaxation and **meditation**.

Flower remedies, flower essences - Although discovered and systematized in the early part of the 20th century by Edward **Bach**, the flower remedies never reached as many people as they have in recent years. Through a simple procedure, using only the dynamic, seed-producing flower of certain non-poisonous plants, the remedy is made. At the height of its blossoming, a flower is placed in a container of water in the sun. The result is that the vibration of the flower is captured in the water. The remedies are used to relieve mental and emotional suffering such as depression, loneliness and fear, as well as problematic attitudes such as lack of confidence or pridefulness.

Dr. Bach did not offer a theory as to why or how the remedies work but did offer much in the way of successful case histories, and the positive proof of the validity of flower remedies continues today. Because the method of preparation is so simple and the results have been so effective and safe, other flower remedies or "essences" as well as "**gem elixirs**" have been developed, expanding beyond Bach's original 38 flower remedies. They have been found quite effective and as Hahnemann, the founder of **homeopathy**, felt, as civilization progresses new diseases are found and new substances and ways of curing these illnesses must be found. See also **Bach, homeopathy.**

Fourth dimension - 1) Described as time/space. 2) Some say the fourth dimension is also part of the etheric world, where thought from the third dimension (our usual reality) exists before it actually takes form on the third dimension. See also **dimensions**.

Free will - The freedom we all have to make choices and decisions for ourselves, regarding our body and our day to day life experiences. What is called the law of free will continues; because each of us has this power of choice, we are all responsible for the decisions we make.

Full moon celebrations, full moon meditations - There are individuals who get together to celebrate the full moon, generally out of doors when possible. These celebrations can take various forms - song, dance, meditation - and the gatherings may not have any specific reason other than to satisfy an inexplicable inner desire to come together. The full moon gatherings have roots in ancient religions where the moon is celebrated as the Goddess of Fertility.

The full moon seems to have a much stronger, more intense effect on the earth than the other phases of the moon. Both tides and people appear to be affected. The term lunatic (derived from "luna" - moon) describes people who exhibit strange behavior during the full moon. Participants in full moon gatherings use this energy to bring strength to their prayers and meditations.

Full spectrum lighting - 1) Natural sunlight. 2) Name given to a type of artificial lighting first developed by Duro-test and called Vita-Lite. This type of light fixture is more energy efficient and lasts longer than the usual kind. Full spectrum lighting also comes much closer to natural sunlight in its color spectrum. There is some evidence that it is more beneficial to live and work in an environment illuminated by a full spectrum light source than one in which only a partial spectrum (such as that produced by normal fluorescent bulbs) is available. See also **color therapy, ELF**.

∞ **G** ∞

Gaia - Also Gaea, in Greek mythology. 1) Gaia is the goddess or supreme being who dates back to pre-Grecian **pagan** times. She is the first goddess, the one who took the world out of chaos and put it in order. Before Apollo, she was the primeval prophetess at Delphi. 2) Gaia is the planet earth. 3) Gaia is popular as a chosen name for women who undergo a **name change** or take a **spiritual name**.

Gem elixirs - Made in the same way as **flower essences** but from gemstones and minerals commonly known as **crystals**. Like flower essences, the elixirs are helpful in bringing about a change in the emotions; however, the effects of the gem elixirs are generally only to the first few bodies of the **aura**. It is felt that the flower essences bring about change in the entire aura.

Genetic encoding - Please see **cell memory**.

Geomancy - 1) The art of divination using natural objects such as stones, shells, sticks or gemstones. The objects are held with a question in mind and then tossed onto the ground. Often there is a drawing on the ground of a divided circle or square. These days, instead of using the ground, some use a piece of paper on the living room floor. The pattern created when the objects fall is interpreted intuitively, generally by a **reader**. As with other **oracles**, the physical objects simply act as a focal point for the reader. 2) Communication with **elementals** for divination or **protection**. 3) The interpretation of natural land forms. See also **feng-shui**.

Give it to the Universe - buzzphrase. Similar to "letting things be what they will" or allowing things to work out in divine order. When you seek an objective or want to **manifest** something, if you give it to the universe, you are actually sending it out into the etheric plane of existence - outside the mental and emotional planes, your immediate sphere. In the etheric plane, the laws of attraction work on the highest spiritual level and you are most likely to bring into your life what is for your **greatest good**.

Goddess - See **goddess energy**.

Goddess energy - buzzphrase. A feeling of being in touch with the highest and most spiritual aspects of the **feminine principle**. It is a feeling which sometimes arises from within and sometimes is evoked from an outside source, such as a special place or person. The ability to sense the goddess energy exists in both men and women. See also **masculine principle**.

Government conspiracy - A number of educated and patriotic U.S. citizens have been uncovering data which seems to indicate that the U.S. government has been withholding information from the general public. This information appears to be mainly focused on subjects such as an **alien** presence on the planet and the possibility of a secret government within our government. Those who believe that there may be such a conspiracy also speculate about the truth we receive concerning our country's international relations and about the possible diversion of scientific information to the detriment of the general public and the economic good of some of our large corporations. Credible people have come forward with information concerning secret government activities. See also **cattle mutilations, implants, Tesla**.

Greatest good - 1) What the higher self seeks as a goal. 2) The best possible outcome of a situation taken from the point of view of the universal plan, which we humans may not be fully aware of. 3) The phrase "if it is for my (or another's) greatest good" may be used after asking that any need or desire be fulfilled. The intention in using this phrase is to insure that what is being asked for would not unknowingly harm anyone.

Great White Brotherhood - A group of high spirit beings who reside on the **etheric plane**. Having had many lifetimes on earth they have perfected themselves and are teachers, helping to guide the progress of civilization on earth. They have remarkable powers and are able to control natural forces on both the etheric and the physical planes. The Great White Brotherhood can bring their messages to us through **channels**. The color "white" refers to the color of light surrounding these beings. Jesus or **Sananda** is currently the Master in charge of the Great White Brotherhood.

Ground, grounded - 1) To bring spiritual truths into our everyday existence. 2) To stay balanced and centered. To maintain an even temper by way of the elimination of excessive energy from the body. Such energy may take many forms such as inappropriate excitement, a clouded mind or anger. See also **center**.

Guided meditation - A leader or guide will, by simply speaking to an individual or a group, bring about a relaxed state of body and mind. The guide's voice is the focal point for the meditation and will direct the individual or the group in using various techniques to consciously relax the body and mind. The goal of the guided meditation might simply be this state of relaxation; however, once this state is reached, the guide could continue to deepen the state of consciousness by creating a fantasy journey, perhaps inside a crystal, perhaps to a peaceful place or even into a **past life regression**. The purposes of a guided meditation are limitless. The guided meditation can be done "live" or can be recorded on audio or video tape. See also **hypnosis, meditation, past life regression, subliminal tapes, visualization**.

Guides - Please see **spirit guides**.

Guru - Sanskrit for "teacher."

∞ **H** ∞

Hands on healing - buzzphrase. Any therapy where the practitioner's touch is a major component of the healing therapy. See also **healing magnetism, reiki, shiatsu**.

Handwriting analysis - Also known as graphology or graphoanalysis. The analyst uses a handwriting sample to interpret personality traits and character. The slant and size of the letters, the loopy or jagged qualities are all clues to the personality.

Harmonic Convergence - For some, the Harmonic Convergence, August 16-17, 1987, signifies the dawn of the New Age. The name was coined and the dates were determined by Jose Arguelles and popularized by those concerned with world peace. These dates were discovered to have been spoken of in the prophecies of a number of ancient cultures in the American continents. In his book *The Mayan Factor*, Arguelles says, "It is a moment for all people of all traditions and ways of life to gather and remember the sacredness which originally consecrated their traditions and their being. Harmonic Convergence is not Armageddon but the avoidance of it. It is a moment to look again at who and what we are as humans together on this planet, of this planet. Through collectively allowing, surrendering and letting go, the higher purposes and priorities of life on earth may imprint and make themselves known as if for the first time."

Harmonic Convergence was celebrated with prayer, meditation and ritual. For many it was a time to recognize that the ability to create a better world lies within themselves rather than in something or someone on the outside. Celebrations on this day continue and many call it "New Age Day."

Hatha yoga - The branch of **yoga** which emphasizes purification and strengthening of the body (the house of the spirit) as the first step toward spiritual perfection. Hatha yoga is sometimes thought of as being the whole system of yoga although it is not. See also **tantra, yoga**.

Healer - buzzword. 1) A person who seems to have some extraordinary ability to heal others. The healer may use a nontraditional method of healing. 2) Many people recognize that we all have the natural ability to heal ourselves and others. Thus, we can all be considered healers. 3) Any person who practices traditional or nontraditional therapies.

Healing, a healing - The moment when relief from an ailment is received. This term usually designates a healing that is less of a physical nature than it is of a spiritual or emotional nature. Healing is thought to be accomplished when the body is brought back into balance through restoring the natural flow of energy in the body. See also **healing at a distance**.

Healing at a distance - Distance is no barrier in the healing process. When the individual who needs a **healing** is not in the presence of the healer, a picture or other personal object, **talisman** or **amulet** can be used to tune in to or locate that person on the **etheric plane** which is where the healing takes place. The healing may affect the physical body as well. When someone is healed only on the physical level, emotional scars sometimes remain. **Healing at a distance** works directly with the non-physical levels.

In order to respect the free will of the person who is in need of healing, the healer always asks permission to do the healing. This permission can be granted on the etheric and the astral levels. If permission is not granted, the healer must abandon the attempt to do the healing. In a situation such as this, the healer must sense or intuit whether or not permission has been granted. See also **akashic records**.

Healing master - One of the **spirit world beings**. The healing master, a discarnate **entity** of highest spiritual intent, may come when asked in order to help a **healer**. The healing master can make his or her presence felt to the healer and will work with the patient directly or through the hands of the healer.

Hellerwork - A technique of deep muscle massage. Done in a series of 11 sessions, Hellerwork releases deep muscle tension which may have built up over a lifetime. It restores good posture and efficient movement. Hellerwork also increases body sensitivity and provides an understanding of how attitudes affect the physical body. Hellerwork assists in exploring an individual's relationship with the body. See also **body memory, bodywork, massage**.

Herbs, herbology - Herbs are plants which lack woody tissue and are valued for their flavors or medicinal properties. Herbology or herbal medicine is the science of using herbs to maintain and restore health. The tradition of using herbs as medicine is quite strong in India, China and Tibet, all of which have developed a considerable amount of literature explaining the theory and practice of herbology. Our European and Native American traditions were less well documented until the 20th century when there was much research in this field.

Although many abandoned herbal research in favor of synthetic drugs, there is a resurgence of interest in herbs because of the undesirable side effects caused by synthetic drugs. This trend is also due to a changing attitude about health and how to maintain it. Herbs are foods and not drugs. Generally speaking, herbs will purify, strengthen, energize or calm and tone the human system, allowing the system to heal itself naturally. See also **naturopathy**.

Higher self - Also known as the superconscious self. 1) The higher self is the part of the mind which can tune in to universal truths. 2) It is the most spiritual part of the mind. See also **channel, manifest.**

Hindu - 1) One who practices Hinduism. 2) With roots in Hinduism or of that religion. The word "Hindu" is Persian for "Indian." During the Persian invasions, the peoples of India were called "Hindu" by outsiders and their religion was then called "Hinduism." Indians call their religion "Santana Dharma," eternal **dharma**.

Hinduism - Practiced mainly in India, Hinduism according to its own mythology is millions of years old. This religion was handed down in an oral tradition until the Vedas, the "knowledge," was written down about 1500-1200 B.C.E. Although Hinduism is considered a polytheistic (many gods and goddesses) religion, it is simultaneously monotheistic (one God). The many gods and goddesses are different aspects of the one God, who is so all-present that the mind cannot grasp it. The many gods and goddesses make it easier to select an aspect of the one God to then identify with and worship.

There are many different sects within Hinduism and even **Buddhism** is a reformed movement of Hinduism.

It would require volumes to properly describe the complexity of Hinduism; however, what is important to understand is that much of the New Age approach to and understanding of spirituality and life has its roots in Hinduism. The New Age has also made a place in the English language for many **Sanskrit** words.

Some of the important teachings of Hinduism that are also found within the New Age are: **Reincarnation** - the soul or spirit has lived before in other bodies and will live again after this body dies. **Karma** - we determine our next lifetime by our actions in the present lifetime. And Maya - that the world we see is illusion and not the true nature of life.

For the **Hindu**, the first spiritual goal is to know his or her spiritual nature and to rediscover the original relationship with God, to reunite with Brahman, the personified god that is "all pervading." Secondly, and most importantly, the goal of the Hindu is to break the chain of action and reaction (karma) and be liberated from the cycle of birth, death and rebirth. This state, nirvana, is the absolute reality beyond what we usually perceive as real.

Hinduism declares that we are a spark of God and that God underlies everything within our perception. This idea is slightly modified in the Buddhist religion and has significant impact within the New Age. Please see **Buddhism** for a more complete discussion.

Holism - From the Greek "holos," "whole," complete, total, all encompassing. 1) In theory, the universe is a living, evolving organism and like the many organisms it contains, it is greater than the sum of its parts. The universe is a complete unit and if any one part is changed, the whole is changed. 2) Energy can never be lost, only rearranged. The whole can be neither increased nor diminished. The life events that we perceive as gain or loss (death, disease, birth, wellness) when viewed in the context of holism, impersonally, without emotion or desire for a particular outcome, are perceived only as movement and change. See also **energy, evolution**.

Holistic - From **holism**: The position that no matter how large or small a part of the universe is, if it is changed there is an effect on the larger unit. This holds true in all cases. For example, a) a diseased kidney will affect the functioning of the whole organism, b) the ill health of an individual affects the entire family unit and even the planet, c) the integrity of our planet affects the universe. See also **holistic health therapies**.

Holistic health therapies - Physical disease is not treated as separate from attitudes, emotions, environment, relationships or lifestyle choices. You and your state of wellness are considered as a whole. All aspects of your being are considered when treating disease. Often a condition is treated from a number of different angles simultaneously. For example, high blood pressure may be treated with medication, **stress** reduction and a change of diet. In holistic health therapies there is an emphasis on returning the client to a proper state of health. For example, the definition of good health for an Olympic athlete is different than for a sixty year old librarian. It's important to realize that the "right" state of health is something determined by the client rather than the health practitioner.

The intention of holistic therapy is to stimulate the individual's natural healing ability to take over the healing processes when they have been blocked or unable to function properly. This approach is based on the idea that every being naturally seeks its own perfect state. See also **evolution**.

Hollow earth - The concept that the earth's center is not, as we are taught in grade school, a core of molten metal, but is hollow and inhabited by a race of beings.

Homeopathy - The name homeopathy is derived from the Greek "homios" which means "similar" or "like." A method of healing systematized by Samuel Hahnemann in the 18th century and based on the **Law of Similars**. To bring about a cure, the homeopathic physician will prescribe minute doses of remedies which, in large doses, would cause the same illness in a healthy individual. The dispensing of these very small doses to someone who is already showing symptoms. intensifies the reaction of the immune system, allowing the body to heal itself. Homeopathy theorizes that the symptoms are not the disease. Rather, they are evidence of disease, and treatment of only the symptoms suppresses the body's natural healing process, thus perpetuating the disease.

Substances specially prepared for this type of healing are called "homeopathics." They are also commonly called "remedies" rather than "medicine." Homeopathy is practiced by physicians and lay people alike. Specific remedies and groups of remedies which relieve many common ailments such as colds, allergies or indigestion are readily available for home use. Homeopathy may be used along with **allopathic** medicine when indicated.

Hook into, hook up - buzzphrase. 1) To send **etheric lines** into the Supreme Intelligence or the earth, or both, for **protection**, to receive information or **grounding** or to **heal at a distance**. 2) Hook into, tap into and **tune into** are synonyms. See also **akashic records**.

Horoscope - Generally refers to the information obtained from an **astrological reading**. See also **astrology**.

Hugs, hug therapy, hugger - Embracing one another upon meeting, when parting or at any other time has become a way for people to show more love and sympathy for one another. Hugging is not just for people who know each other well. Those who are avid huggers will embrace on the first meeting. Hug therapy says that the best prescription for what ails you could be a little more human contact with a dash of brotherly love.

Hypnosis - The technique of bringing someone into a state of mental and physical relaxation. Hypnosis allows an individual to bypass potentially inhibiting conscious control in order to connect with some deeper awareness. The practice of hypnosis is known as hypnotherapy.

∞ I ∞

I AM - The divine spark of **Spirit** that is all people. "I AM," it is said by the "I AM" Religious Activity of Saint Germaine Foundation, to be the "Great Creative Word, God in Action." See also **co-create, OM.**

I Ching - *The Book of Changes.* Ancient Chinese book (2500-1150 B.C.E.) of divination. Much more than a book of fortune telling, the *I Ching* (pronounced ee-ching) will handle a question for those who ask by first clarifying the situation asked about and then giving guidelines for correct conduct in the situation.

To get a response from the *I Ching*, toss three coins simultaneously. (Yarrow sticks were used in ancient times.) The sides of the coins are designated as **yin** or **yang**, soft or firm. Each toss of the coins will result in a predominantly yin or predominantly yang number of sides. The result is translated into an unbroken line (yang) or a broken line (yin). By tossing the coins six times, a hexagram (six lines) made of two tri-grams (three lines each) is created. All possible combinations of the two types of lines add up to 64 different hexagrams. The *I Ching* comments on all 64 hexagrams, from number one, "before completion" to number sixty four, "after completion," through the full cycle of changes.

Illumination, illumined - The conscious realization that there is a spark within us that is divine, perfect and eternal.

Immune system - The natural ability of the body to protect itself from disease.

Implant - A small device placed into the physical or **etheric body** of a human being by **ET's**. This implant acts as a receiver and when **activated**, sends information to the human being through the implant. This information can be in the form of instructions, such as where to live or what kind of work to do. These instructions may not seem to have been generated from outside the mind of the person "implanted" but an implant may be suspected if one's goals change suddenly or for no understandable reason. The purpose of these implants is not completely known. People who have been visited by alien beings, those who have seen a space ship at close range or have visited a space ship, are possible candidates for having received an implant. Other good candidates are those who have great interest in **UFO**'s. See also **government conspiracy**.

Incarnate -   1) Having substance or form. A living being. 2) To take form. To be born.

Incarnation - 1) The process of taking on a physical form. 2) Birth. 3) A particular lifetime. See also **reincarnation**.

Initiate - 1) A person who has joined a spiritual group and is in the first stages of learning about the new spiritual path. 2) In ancient Egyptian times, one who followed a path of rigorous spiritual training and passed certain tests.

Inner child - Please see **child within**.

Inner peace - A state of being in which one lives in balance, harmony and happiness. This state is not dependent on other people or material things. The outer world can neither give this peaceful state of being, nor can it take it away.

Intent - The determined and focused direction of will to a particular purpose.

Intuit - To use one's sensitivity to receive information through **intuition**.

Intuition - A knowing of information that comes from inside oneself and not from learning or observation of something outside oneself. Intuition can be described as a "gut feeling."

Involution - The descent of spirit toward the earth. Once on the earth the process reverses itself and becomes **evolution** or an unfolding upward.

Iridology - The study of the eyes, particularly the iris, as a way of discovering disease within the body. The different areas of the iris correspond to different parts of the body. Blotches of color in the iris indicate a weakness or congestion of the corresponding part of the body. Iridology can also show where the strengths of a body lie. See also **reflexology**.

∞ **J** ∞

Jung, Carl - One of the founding fathers of psychotherapy. He wrote extensively on the nature of consciousness, our inner workings and its relationship to our behavior. Jung studied philosophy and religion from around the world and synthesized much of this knowledge into his work. He also brought a westernized understanding to eastern religion and thought.

∞ K ∞

Kabalah - Esoteric Hebrew tradition which teaches the relationship of the spiritual world to the material world. The Kabalah holds the keys to the creative process. It is thought that these teachings were handed down from ancient Egyptian times. The information is presented in the form of an inverted tree, which is why the Kabalah is known as "the tree of life." Symbolism is used to impart this information through numbers, letters, language and geometry. It is thought that the Kabalah is the source of **tarot cards** as well as **numerology**. There are many accepted spellings including **Cabbala, Kabbala, Quabalah, Quaballah**.

Kali - The terrible and frightful **Hindu** goddess of destruction. Kali is one aspect of **Shakti**, the primal female energy. Kali means "black" and "time." Kali brings famine, disease, war and violence. The image of Kali is truly terrible as she dances on corpses and wears a garland of skulls around her neck. She is also known as the "one with a severed head" and as she dances she holds her own decapitated head. She destroys and yet is honored as "Mother of the World." See also **feminine principle**.

Kali yuga - The last of the four "yugas" or ages, in Indian religion. The first age is of truth. The second of knowledge, the third of ritualism and the fourth and final yuga is the Kali yuga, the age of lawlessness. We are currently in the last part of the Kali yuga. At the end of the ages,

Shiva, the **Hindu** god of destruction, will destroy the world so that it might begin again as the first age did, in truth. See also **Kali, tantra.**

Karma - Sanskrit. Karma is the strict, impersonal, universal law of cause and effect. The cause of a particular effect may be an action, a thought or a desire. Even desires which are of value are still desires and they keep one bound to the wheel of karma, the cycle of life, death and rebirth. One of the least recognized aspects of karma is that it is **non-judgmental.** It is the human **ego** which applies labels such as "good" and "bad." Often the New Ager understands karma only as the undesirable result of cause and effect, calling anything bad that happens "karma." Karma is neither good nor bad; it is the result of previous action. The phrase "What goes around, comes around," expresses the law of karma in a way that most Westerners understand. See also **contract, Hinduism, lesson.**

Karmic relationship - A relationship with a history in past lifetimes. Such relationships occur for many reasons. There may be things which need to be worked out in the current lifetime. Perhaps one party in the relationship has **lessons** to learn and can only progress on life's path by learning these lessons in this particular relationship. Perhaps all close relationships are karmic, for it is through our relationships, not our intellect, that we live life and learn. As with **karma** itself, many people say a relationship is "karmic" only when it is difficult and filled with struggle and not when it is easy and filled with love. See also **"connection to," karma.**

Kinesiology - Please see **muscle testing**.

Kirlian photography - Developed by Russians Semyon and Valentina Kirlian about 1939. This type of photography allows the study of changes in the **electromagnetic field** or **aura** as a way of diagnosing illness. Kirlian and a fellow scientist, Burr, found dramatic changes in the electromagnetic field in the presence of diseases like cancer. Kirlian photography uses the process of electrophotography to capture an image of the energy of life on a film emulsion.

Kundalini - **Hindu** in origin. Also plays a small part in Buddhism. Kundalini is a mysterious energy associated with fire and said to live in everyone. Kundalini is likened to a snake lying coiled at the base of the spine, within the area of the first or root **chakra**. Kundalini is considered to be female in nature. It is thought by some that this energy does not exist until the aspirant concentrates on this area and creates this energy with his or her mind. This type of meditation can take years of practice, although some believe that the energy lies dormant, waiting to activate in its own time. See also **kundalini yoga, tantra, yoga**.

Kundalini yoga - A series of elaborate techniques, known as tantric exercises, which awaken the **kundalini** energy and cause it to ignite. This **energy** works its way upward through the body and unites with the sahasrara, or crown **chakra**, at the top of the head; and this union brings about Supreme Bliss or the Great Awakening.

Law of Similars - "Like is cured by like." As described by ancient Hindu **sages** and as written by Hippocrates in 400 B.C.E., "Through the like, disease is produced and through the application of the like, it is cured." As used in **homeopathy** - a remedy is chosen for a patient by matching symptoms to a remedy which, in larger doses, would produce the same symptoms in a healthy person. See also **Bach.**

Learning experience - buzzphrase. 1) From the perspective that life on earth is like time spent in a schoolroom and that we are here to learn, every experience we have is an opportunity to learn something about ourselves. From this learning, we progress along the path of perfection. 2) "Learning experience" can be a more positive expression for "painful experience," whether an attempt at learning from the situation is made or not. See also **evolution, lesson, reason.**

Left-brain - 1) The hemisphere of the brain which is said to control linear thought and facts, such as mathematics, as differentiated from the right hemisphere which relates to our creative and non-linear nature. 2) buzzword. Someone could be called "left brained" meaning perhaps, that he or she is a stickler for facts or likes to do things by the "letter of the law." As a compliment, it could mean that the person is excellent at paperwork or details. 3) A task may be described as "left-brained," meaning that it requires concentration on facts or details. See also **right brain**.

Lemuria - A continent thought to be located where the Indian Ocean is now. Lemuria is known to us primarily through **channels**. Lemurians, the inhabitants of Lemuria, are said to have come from different race roots than human beings today. Some believe that the Lemurian culture pre-dates that of **Atlantis** by millions of years. Others think the two cultures co-existed and that it was the rivalry between them that led them to destruction. The Atlanteans are thought to have been culturally superior to the Lemurians, since Atlantis was a culture of a scientifically oriented nature and Lemuria of a more philosophical nature. Both Atlantis and Lemuria are thought to have been outposts for visitors from other planets and star systems and some think that Lemuria is the same as the continent of Mu. Others believe Mu to have been a different continent which was also submerged and lost. See also **Atlantis**.

Lesson, life lessons - buzzword. Similar to **learning experience**. Lessons come through the challenges that life brings. When the person being challenged has not yet mastered the situation in a satisfying way, it is said that he or she is learning a lesson.

Ley lines - Unseen lines of electromagnetic energy which form a grid around the planet. These lines can be detected by sensitive people through divining techniques such as **dowsing** and **geo-**

mancy. Electromagnetism covers the earth in a way that is little understood at this time. Possibly these lines carry a slightly greater concentration of energy than the rest of the planet.

There are two types of ley lines. The first is a man made road or path which leads to or connects important landmarks. The second exists in nature first and may have inspired the placement of ancient landmarks such as Stonehenge in England, the pyramids of Egypt and other markers such as obelisks and temples. It is thought that these sites were chosen for placement of landmarks with the full knowledge that the power of the ley line would amplify the power of the pyramid or temple.

Ley lines have special powers attributed to them, with different ley lines seeming to amplify the human experience in subtly different ways. Human intent can also affect ley lines. When two ley lines intersect, what is called a ley center or power spot is created. This convergence of lines may be what is experienced at "**vortexes**." See also **feng-shui**.

Life path - buzzphrase. The direction and purpose of one's life. Life has been described as a road or path in many different cultures throughout time.

Light - 1) Light is the presence of God. It is the ultimate healer and cleanser. The sun, our only source of light, has been the focus of worship for societies throughout history. 2) buzzword. To "send (someone) light," "**surround (it) in light**," to "be in the light." Light is associated with the highest principles, thoughts and everything of great spiritual value.   See also **candles, light worker, violet flame.**

Light being - A very highly evolved **spirit being.** See also **spirit world beings.**

Light worker - Someone with a high level of commitment to personal and planetary spiritual development, to peace and the ending of suffering on the planet.   The light worker interacts with unseen forces in the world. For the light worker there is much **meditation** and communication with **guides, spirit teachers** and **healing masters.**   Often, to help the planet, thoughts of love and **light** are sent to the planet or to those around the world who are in need.   Some light workers call themselves **metaphysicians.**

Limitations - buzzword.   A person's faults or shortcomings.

Lucid dreaming - A technique which requires training yourself to be aware that you are dreaming while you are dreaming. Once aware of the dream state, you can then learn to shape the dream. You can then travel anywhere you want to go, meet with people you would like to meet, use the dream state to find creative solutions to challenges you might not otherwise find, gain insights into daily problems and overcome fears. For some, lucid dreaming is a way of learning how to control **astral travel.** Also called conscious dreaming.   See also **Eckankar.**

∞ **M** ∞

Magnetism, healing magnetism - Also known as vital force, animal magnetism or Od. Not to be confused with **healing with magnets** or magnetic fields. There are indications that the ancient Egyptians and Greeks used this healing technique. It was further developed by Paracelsus in the early 16th century and Franz Anton Mesmer and Carl von Reichenbach in the 18th century.

Magnetic healing is based on the fact that the human system has a vital life force which can be transferred to another person to aid in the healing process. We are all born with this magnetism. It is the animating force in our bodies. It can be transferred based on the magnetic principle that opposites attract. When transferring magnetism to another, the left hand of the healer will work on the right side of the receiver and the right hand on the left side.

There are two basic healing methods called positive and negative. The positive is used when the patient is fatigued and therefore low in vital force. The negative method is used when the patient is in pain or when there is excitement and an excess of magnetism is present. The positive calls for a transference of magnetism to the body and the negative calls for a drawing off of magnetism. Both methods help to bring about a harmonious distribution of the life force in the human system, bringing it back into balance.

Magnets, healing with - Based on the fact that we are constantly exposed to low level magnetic fields, this healing technique makes use of the effects of magnetic fields as generated from natural or man-made magnets on the living system. Through the direct application of small **bio-magnets** or other larger more powerful magnets to the body, the body is exposed to either the north (south seeking) pole or the south (north seeking) pole of the magnet. Each pole has a distinct quality of energy. The north pole has a negative energy and a negative, slowing, arresting effect on biological organisms. The south pole has a positive energy, improving growth, stimulating energy flow. In choosing which pole to apply for healing, it is important to understand the root of the illness as well as the actions of the two different poles. In cases of bacteria, inflammation and pain, the north pole is used. In case of pain due to muscle weakness or contraction of muscles or organs, the south pole is used.

Male, male energy, masculine principle - 1) The positive aspect of the universe as opposed to the negative. The positive qualities (in terms of energy) are described as intellectual and active. The positive, or male, is associated with spirit rather than the earth and the sun rather than the moon. 2) In the **mystical** study of the universe, there is constant interaction between the male and the female principles, creating a natural balance where one principle never completely dominates. The **Piscean Age** is said to be characterized by an overabundance of male energy which can be balanced by bringing more **female energy** into our lives as we move into the **Age of Aquarius**. It is this imbalance which has created

our current world situation. See also **female,
Piscean Age, witchcraft, yang, yin.**

Manifest - buzzword. As one of the usual definitions indicates, to manifest is to materialize or
exteriorize. 1) For the New Ager, manifesting
something goes like this: The process starts
with the thought of what is to be manifested.
Visualization is used to strengthen the thought
process. The **visualization** is repeated daily for
varying numbers of days, sometimes with the
help of a **crystal** or other item whose purpose is
to help focus the energy. The thought is then
put out into the universe.

For example: If you need a new car, you
create an image of, or **visualize**, the car in your
mind; perhaps it is in front of your house or you
are driving or washing it. Then you hold the
image in your mind for a while. This process is
repeated over several days. At the end of each
day's visualization, you could say something like,
"If it is for my **greatest good** . . ." and then
forget about it until the next day. 2) Sometimes
manifestation occurs without the use of any kind
of specific exercises. What is needed simply appears or occurs. An example of this is when just
the right person, job or object becomes available
at just the right moment. We usually relate this
idea to the good things that come to us but it can
also relate to the trying people and times we **attract to** ourselves. See also **karma.**

Mantra - One of the original, universal sounds
or a specific set of these sounds, as found in the
Sanskrit language. When one of these sounds is
repeated mentally, aloud or in writing, it will

bring the vibration of that sound into the body, mind and spirit. Repetition of a mantra in a specific way is called "japa," one form of **yoga** and is one of the most direct ways to purify the mind and spirit leading to self-realization or enlightenment. Mantra has come to mean a word or phrase which is repeated, acting as a focal point for the mind, to aid in relaxation or **meditation**.

Massage - Rubbing of the body primarily to reduce tension in the muscles. Massage has come a long way from the days of the "rub down." There are many techniques ranging from the deep muscle work of Rolfing and Swedish massage to the whisper light touch of lymphatic massage. If you will be having a massage, talk with the person doing the work to see if the technique suits you. A massage generally lasts anywhere from 30 to 90 minutes. See also **Alexander method, alternative therapies, bodywork, Hellerwork**.

Master - 1) One who has found great spiritual knowledge and put this knowledge into practice in his or her own life. One who has found balance in the physical, mental, emotional and spiritual aspects of life. 2) A person of authority who leads others in a path of knowledge.

Material plane - A synonym for the earth plane, our physical reality, life on earth.

Medicine - Borrowed from the Native American culture, medicine is anything that is good for you. It can be good for health, **protection**, bringing good fortune. Each person's medicine is individualized to his or her own needs.

Medicine bag or pouch - Originally used by some tribes of the Native American culture, the medicine bag is a pouch usually worn around the waist or neck. The contents of the medicine pouch would vary greatly from tribe to tribe. Sometimes parts of animals, roots, herbs or **crystals** were carried. The New Age community has adopted the medicine bag in its own way. Empty the pocket or purse of any New Ager and chances are you will find a medicine pouch. The pouch will probably contain crystals or other stones and some form of **amulet** or **talisman**.

Medicine wheel - The medicine wheel has its origins in the Plains Indian culture of North America. A circle of stones, the wheel represents the circle of life. It is used for prayer, meditation, teaching and learning. A medicine wheel found in the high country of Wyoming, the Bighorn Medicine Wheel, is a good indicator that the wheel was also used as an astronomical tool. On Summer Solstice, the sun rises in alignment with the center of the wheel and the spokes of the wheel mark solar and stellar alignments.

The wheel is constructed outdoors and is oriented to the four primary directions, each of which is represented by certain qualities, colors and animals. Ceremonies using the medicine wheel can be fairly simple or very elaborate with many days preparation and many participants.

The use of the circle or wheel is found in many cultures. It seems to be a common way of representing the cyclical nature of life.

Meditation - The science and practice of deep concentration and contemplation. Meditation can take many forms ranging from the classical and very specific techniques practiced in the **Hindu** and **Buddhist** traditions to the New Age practice of the meditation circle. Meditation can be done in private for specific personal spiritual development or, in its more public forms, can be used for a common goal; for example, a meditation on peace. A meditation of this type is meant to strengthen the thought being meditated upon, trusting that it will become reality. Classically, meditation is used to empty the mind of earthly thoughts and desires in order to bring the meditator to **enlightenment**. See also **guided meditation, manifest**.

Meditation tapes - 1) Pre-recorded audio tapes which create an atmosphere conducive to **meditation**. These tapes are generally recordings of music using such instruments as pianos, synthesizers, harps, flutes, bells and gongs. The music is very soothing and many meditation tapes are composed in a way which induces a brain wave frequency of 60 cycles per second which is characteristic of meditation. 2) A cassette tape that features a **guided meditation**.

Meridian lines - An ancient Chinese concept. There are invisible lines or channels which carry subtle energy known as "nerve fluid" throughout the body and connect the organs to each other. See also **acupuncture**.

Metaphysician - One who has studied the nature of life beyond the physical plane. A metaphysician in the New Age sense might be a **channel**, a **healer**, one who works with the unseen forces of nature for the benefit of others and the planet. Can be synonymous with **light worker**.

Metaphysics - The study of natural phenomena generally thought of as being outside the scope of sciences such as geology, physics or chemistry. Metaphysics makes use of philosophy, scientific method and intuition in order to gain an understanding of the laws of the universe beyond the physical plane. See also **intuition**.

Michael - 1) One of the four archangels. Michael is the overseer of the physical realm. 2) A very high spirit being who sometimes communicates with human beings through **channels**. Many people channel Michael. His personality and information seem to vary from channel to channel and to be colored by the personality of the channel. Michael is said to be the sponsor of the **Ashtar Command**. See also **contract**.

Mirror - buzzword. Observing your reaction to another person's behavior can provide great insight into your own behavior. When someone else's behavior irritates you, that person may be "mirroring" one of your own behavior patterns - a pattern of which you are completely unconscious; and, if you were conscious of it, would not like it. Because you would not like the behavior in yourself, when you see it in someone else, you react with anger or irritation.

A "mirror" can also be someone in whom you perceive similarities with yourself and whose response in a given situation provides a teaching for you in how to handle a similar situation in your life. See also **non-judgmental, karma.**

Mission, life mission - buzzword. The particular reason for one's life in relation to other people, one's own spiritual development and the planet. Since nothing happens randomly and there is a purpose for every event in life, even if it is not clearly understood at the time, it stands to reason that everyone would have a mission, a reason for **incarnating.** See also **reason.**

Moon - Relates to qualities of the **feminine principle.** Reflective, emotional, intuitive in nature.

Moon sign - In **astrology,** your moon sign is the sign of the **zodiac** the moon was in at the moment of your birth. This sign gives insight into your emotional makeup and the past life lessons which are to be dealt with in this lifetime.

Mu - Please see **Lemuria.**

Muscle testing - A method of using an isolated muscle to obtain data about the organs and functions of the body on emotional, nutritional, energetic and structural levels. When you hold or touch an object or think about an idea, a second person can test you in the following manner: Hold your arm straight out in front of you at shoulder height. If the arm can be easily pressed down, the muscle is indicating a negative response, a "no" answer. If the muscle remains strong, it indicates a positive response, a "yes" answer. Helpful in decision making and selecting remedies. Also known as kinesiology.

Mystic - A person who brings spiritual knowledge and truth forward through **psychic** skills rooted in a religious background. A person who seeks to experience God directly. A mystic can also be known as a psychic.

Mystical experience - 1) An experience of lasting value which is sometimes described as enlightenment. A direct experience of God through which there is a transcendence of the material world and a momentary understanding of the eternal. 2) A religious or spiritual event that can change one's life forever. See also **shift**.

∞ **N** ∞

Nada - Hindu, Sanskrit. Female facet of **Shakti**. See also **female principle, negative, yin**.

Nadis - An invisible network of nerve canals located in the **astral body**. They connect to the physical body at the base of the spine and run throughout the body. Similar to **meridian lines**. See also **acupuncture**.

Name changes - Changing your given name has become popular within the New Age community. Taking a **spiritual name** as part of an initiation into a religion or brotherhood is as old as religion itself. However, there are additional reasons for name changes in the New Age. Some of them are: a) The notion that in changing your name, you can change your destiny. Alternate names are sometimes chosen using **numerology**. b) Your **spirit guides** or a **reader** may tell you the name of your **spirit**, which is different from your given name. Taking on this spirit name is said to bring you closer to your true nature. c) Maybe you are a **walk-in** and feel that continuing to use your birth name is uncomfortable or inappropriate.

Native American culture - There has been enormous interest in the Native American culture, especially in spiritual practices. This interest has focused primarily on the idea that the Native American culture has something to teach at this time when so many are concerned about the eco-

logy and our relationship with the earth. Traditionally, Native Americans have felt that they are
the custodians or caretakers of the earth, rather
than her owners and exploiters. Many Native
Americans welcome and encourage non-native
participation in their ceremonies hoping to bring
the peoples of the world closer together and to
help foster a gentler attitude toward the earth.
Because of these feelings toward the land, any
object representing the Native American culture
has become a symbol to many for having a closer
relationship with the land.

There are those who are interested in the
ongoing struggle of the Native American with
the U.S. government over land and treaties
which guarantee the Native Americans their
freedom of religion. See also **ritual**.

Nature spirits - See **Elementals**.

Naturopathy, naturopathic - Method of promot-
ing wellness using natural substances. There is
emphasis on fresh air, lots of sunshine and good
nutrition. The naturopath is not necessarily
interested in stopping the disease but in helping
it run its natural course as quickly and as
comfortably as possible. Herbal remedies and
homeopathics might be used; however, the use of
synthetic drugs is discouraged.

Near death experience - What has become
known as the "near death experience," or NDE,
is a result of a variety of life threatening experiences. Many of these NDE's are recounted by
those who have come back to life after being
declared dead by professional health technicians

or doctors, people who are unlikely to make a mistake in such a declaration.

There are some differences in the NDE stories; however, the similarities are striking. Every person reports having seen a light, as if at the end of a corridor. Each also tells of a feeling of indescribable peace and love which seems to come from this light. And each reports a strong desire to go toward the light. On this trip toward the light, deceased friends and relatives are often visible, welcoming and at peace.

During this experience there is the realization or instruction from "somewhere out there" that it is not time to continue toward the light. Each person is reluctant to turn back because the light feels so beautiful and loving, but obviously, each one does.

Afterwards, common experiences are: the feeling of greater peace in life, renewed or new found feelings of spirituality and a loss of the fear of death. Many who have had an NDE have spoken publicly about the experience in the hope of reassuring others that death is only a **transition** and not the end of life.

Negative - 1) come to mean - A qualitative assessment from a particular point of view; something unhappy or unpleasant, not beneficial. 2) Also describes the "negative" or South magnetic pole. 3) In the ancient eastern religions, the **female** aspect of the universe, **yin** (Chinese) and **nada** (Hindu) concepts. See also **female principle.**

Negative ions - Ions, electrically charged particles, have either a positive or a negative charge.

It has been demonstrated that moods are affected by the atmosphere. Some of the affects are attributed to the ion charge in the area. It is negative ions which induce feelings of well-being and elation. Negative ions are in high concentration at a waterfall or the beach or in a cave and are at a low concentration right before a rainfall. The concentration rises as the rain begins to fall. There are small appliances available commercially which generate negative ions.

Neo-pagan - Please see **pagan**.

New Age - 1) This phrase refers to the **Age of Aquarius** or Aquarian age. 2) New Age is an ambiguous umbrella term for assorted groups, religions and ideas most of which are new to us in the West. See also **Age of Aquarius, Harmonic Convergence, Introduction**.

New Age music - P.J. Birosik, author of *The New Age Music Guide* (Macmillan), describes New Age music (NAM), as so diverse that "thirteen sub-genre" have been created for it. NAM can be characterized by its tendency to be calming with little variation in tempo and beat throughout a piece. Although the music has been mostly instrumental in the past, vocals are now being introduced. NAM, in general, is not the kind of music whose melody will stick in your mind. Generally, it is relaxing and conducive to the **meditative** state. However, some of the music has definite jazzy overtones.

There are those who see NAM as "world music" because of its use of the music of other cultures, music quite unfamiliar to many of us in the West - drums of Africa, the bell and cymbal of Tibet, the flute of the Native American cultures. Some musicians have used scale systems which are unfamiliar to western ears. Others have incorporated subliminal messages to help in the healing process or change unproductive behavior patterns. Some musicians maintain that sound, rhythms, particular notes and certain progressions of notes have a profound influence on the human system. These composers create music for specific purposes. NAM is a rapidly growing field and as of early 1992 has captured more than 5% of the music market.

New ending - A technique or **tool** used by some **healers** and therapists to help release undesirable behavior patterns or change responses to certain situations. The technique can be used to relieve recurring nightmares, unreasonable anxiety in specific situations or the pain of past experiences.

For example, recurring nightmares can be stopped quite effectively with the assistance of a therapist who helps the dreamer give the dream a new ending. The dreamer is asked to recount the dream until the uncomfortable part comes up. The dreamer is then asked to create the dream's "new ending." The intent is that the new ending will take over when the dream recurs.

The technique is quite effective - perhaps because the dreamer actually makes up the new ending rather than using suggestions made by others. Somehow, consciously providing a positive ending for the fantasy puts the unpleasantness to rest. This technique is also known as rewriting.

NLP, Neuro-Linguistic Programming - A technique which helps in understanding our own behavior and that of others by paying attention to language and physical mannerisms. NLP can provide insight into how an individual perceives the world and organizes it in the mind. NLP is a **tool** which can be used to change negative attitudes and behaviors in both the conscious and subconscious minds through a change in language. See also **affirmations**.

Non-judgmental - buzzword. Often heard in New Age circles. Being non-judgmental of another's actions means acceptance of another without opinion. To act in a non-judgmental way permits freedom from the negativity and anger which can be generated by judging. Since the Universe does not judge, reward or punish, being non-judgmental of others allows the principles of the Universe to flow more easily. Quite often the New Ager finds that to be non-judgmental is quite a challenge and can provide an important lesson in the progression toward a more perfect state. See also **karma**.

Non-ordinary reality - See **shaman, shamanism**.

Nutritional Therapy - The process of correcting illness or disease by adding a particular food to or eliminating it from the diet. Nutritional therapy is exceptionally successful in treating allergies. Food choices are made specifically for the individual. Frequently, other therapies are used in conjunction with nutritional therapy. There are a number of **tools** available to the nutritional therapist for determining how the diet should be changed. Among them are **muscle testing**, use of a **pendulum**, study of the present diet and chemical analysis of the hair. A hair analysis will indicate which minerals the body has and what is lacking. The therapist can then prescribe the proper vitamins, minerals and other food supplements to be used and recommend an individualized diet plan. See also **ayurvedic medicine, herbs, naturopathy**.

Numerology - The study of numbers can be traced back to Pythagoras and the **Kabalah**. Numbers and letters have **vibrations**. An individual's name can be given a numerical value and that, along with the birth date, provides the numerologist with definite clues to the present life. The numerologist can track events in past lives and, in so doing, provide insights into relationships and events in this life.

The study of numbers provides insight into major life patterns and shows how the soul chooses to work with them. Some of these major patterns are: cooperation with self and others, expression and communication, work on the spiritual self, work on the material self and creativity.

Old Age - 1) Refers to the **Piscean Age**, the age we are leaving for the new **Aquarian Age**. 2) An outmoded way of doing something, for example: relating to others, doing business, treating oneself. 3) The term **Old Age** brings with it connotations of greed, war, deceit, environmentally unsound practices, etc.

OM - Sanskrit. Ancient eastern roots. Although also spelled Aum, OM is the generally preferred spelling in the West. The primal sound of the universe. The sound from which all sounds originate. There is no  translation of OM. The sound of OM is A, U, M. Esoterically, "A" represents the physical plane, "U," the mental or astral plane, "M," the deep sleep state and all that is beyond the rational mind. When repeated, the sound will bring great peace to the one repeating it. Over time, when repeated frequently and correctly, OM will have profound strengthening effects on the physical body as well as the mental powers. OM can be used as a **mantra** or part of a mantra, a **chant** or as a closing to a **meditation**.

On all levels - buzzphrase. If a therapy claims to heal you "on all levels," the therapy will heal you on the physical plane, the emotional plane, the mental plane and the **etheric plane** (all pertaining to the **aura**). Put in less esoteric terms, the mind, body and soul.

One Hundredth Monkey - A charming story written by Ken Keyes, Jr. The story is often referred to as an illustration of **synchronicity**, the phenomenon of similar ideas popping up all over the world at the same time. For further description see **synchronicity**.

Oracle - 1) Originally, one who served as a go-between for the **spirit world** and another seeking insight into the future in the form of prophecy. 2) come to mean - One of the **tools** a **psychic** might use to arrive at the information sought by another. There are many such tools: **I Ching**, **runes**, **tarot cards**.

Out of body experience - See **astral travel**.

∞ **P** ∞

Pagan, neo-pagan - "Pagan" was a name given to all animistic religions - religions which worshipped many gods and goddesses or spirits. Paganism was either wiped out by or assimilated into Judeo-Christianity. What is today called **witchcraft** or pagan is recreated from remaining fragments of ancient religions.

Some of these fragments which have been assimilated into Christianity are alive in the present forms of Easter and Christmas. Easter is the celebration of Spring Equinox and the awakening of fertility of the land. Christmas is celebrated at the time that paganism celebrated Winter Solstice and shares similar customs such as gift giving.

The ancient pagan religions of the northern European and Celtic peoples were left more intact than many others. Various groups which have revived some of the aspects of ancient religions are called pagan, neo-pagan or wicca.

Within the various groups, there are different focuses. Some recognize the balance of power between the **male** and **female principles** and strive in their **rituals** and **ceremonies** to bring this balance into the world.

Others seek to once again focus more intensely on the Goddess, thus bringing the pendulum full swing from a predominantly God-centered society with a masculine orientation, to a Goddess-centered society with a feminine orientation, in the hopes that in the future we will find our balance.

In general, the groups are made up of gentle, nature loving people who have chosen these religions because they feel more attracted to the ancient western roots than to the culturally foreign roots of eastern spirituality. See also **witchcraft, yin-yang symbol.**

Palmistry - Palmistry practiced well can present many insights into your personality, health and talents, as well as the past, present and possibilities for the future. 1) Palmistry is an **oracle**, in which the palm of the client is a point of focus for the palmist's **psychic** powers. 2) The palmist (the one who practices palmistry) bases the reading on the hands of the client. By looking at shape, color, texture and lines in the hands and wrists, the palmist can interpret individual characteristics and give insights into the client's life.

Parapsychology - The study of the invisible world of "psi" energies using the scientific method. This includes the study and measurement of **ESP** and other **psychic** talents as well as attempts to explain ghosts and other phenomena in scientific terms.

Past life, past life memory - The memory of having lived before as a particular personality in a particular place and time. See also **past life regression, reincarnation.**

Past life connection - Deep empathy or sympathy with a person, object, place or way of life for which there is no known reason in the present lifetime. The assumption is that there must have been a strong relationship at some point in a past life. This connection can be recognized in a number of ways: through **intuition**, through an inexplicable feeling that it is so, as a result of a **reading** or by an experience during a **past life regression**. See also **cosmic connection, karmic relationship**.

Past life regression - Using **hypnosis** or suggestion, you can be **regressed** or taken back to a point in time before your birth. Past life memories are not limited to earth incarnations. They can also be of the times between incarnations and of lifetimes on other planets.

One of the first popular transcriptions of such a regression was published in the 1940's and was entitled *The Search for Bridey Murphy*. It was ground breaking work by a psychiatrist with a client who, under hypnosis, remembered many past lives. As the subject was "remembering," she felt she was actually a different personality living at a different time. Although there is some dispute as to the authenticity of this work and others like it, Bridey Murphy's story is still a classic recounting of the process of past life regression and of how this information is experienced by the person under hypnosis.

Past life regression can bring insight into various obstacles or **limitations** in the present lifetime. Areas where this insight can be valuable include relationships with relatives or friends, emotional difficulties and phobias which defy understanding within the context of the current lifetime. This **tool** can also be used to shed light upon the more positive aspects of a lifetime, the loves and talents. Perhaps a **regression** can help bring about a better understanding of the choices, challenges and talents presented "this time around."

Pegasus - The winged horse who carried Bellerophon to victory over the fire breathing Chimera in Greek mythology. **Pegasus** seems to represent freedom, strength and wisdom.

Pendulum - A string or chain with a weighted object on one end. The unweighted end is held between the thumb and index finger leaving the object free to swing in any direction. A pendulum is used for communication between an individual's **subconscious** and the unseen energy field of an object. The pendulum can also respond to questions, thus acting as an **oracle**.

Before using the pendulum, the meaning of each of its movements must be established. The pendulum will swing left to right, backward and forward or in circles - clockwise and counterclockwise. Each of these sets of movements represents "yes" and "no" answers to questions. Once the "yes" and "no" responses have been established, almost any kind of question can be asked and answered. Also known as radionics and radiesthesia.

Pentacle - A five pointed star with no additional symbols or writing has been found on pottery from Ur, Sumer and ancient Babylonia. It is also thought to have been inscribed on Solomon's ring and known as the Seal of Solomon. A

pentacle does not necessarily have five equal sides. See also **pentagram**.

Pentagram - A five pointed star whose sides are of equal length, sometimes enclosed within a circle, and perhaps inscribed with magical writing inside the star and around the circle. Consider- ed to be a powerful symbol used in ritual or for **pro-**  **tection**. When there is one point at the top, the symbol is considered upright, warding off evil and bringing good influences. Reversed, two points upward, the pentagram is thought to bring bad influences and is considered the symbol of evil. See also **pentacle**.

Personal power - On a tangible level, personal power is the self-confidence, integrity and ability to create what is desired for physical and emo- tional comfort. On a less tangible level, personal power is described as charisma or talent.

On a **mystical** level, this power can be de- scribed as the ability to enlist the assistance of **entities** to bring desires into reality. There is a lot of talk about personal power in the New Age, how to develop it, how not to give it up to others. Personal power is used in the process of **mani- festation**, creating **protection**, creating **amulets** and **talismans** and is the aspect of a person which enables the successful focusing of **intent**.

Piscean Age - The astrological sign the planet earth is now leaving. See also **Age of Aquarius**.

Polarity - 1) The state of having opposite qualities, powers or poles. 2) Created by Randolph
Stone, a therapy which combines western **chiropractic** methods with eastern **ayurvedic** medicine. The polarity practitioner aligns the
polarity energy of the body by first identifying
areas where the **energy** flow of the human system is misaligned or **blocked**. The practitioner
then uses polarity **bodywork** techniques to release these blocks and allow the energy to move
and find its own point of balance.

This alignment of energy takes place in all
the bodies - physical, emotional, mental and
spiritual. Polarity opens blocks and sometimes
brings them into the conscious mind of the
patient. Once they are in the conscious mind,
the therapist, working with the **aura**, can help
heal the thoughts as well as the physical body.

Pole shift - Literally the shifting of the earth's
magnetic poles. This shift could be as much as
180 degrees - a complete flip of the poles - or
only 90 degrees - which would bring the poles
into the position of the equator. A scientific
study of this phenomenon was pioneered by
Hugh Auchincloss Brown. This theory is based
upon facts that other scientists know to be true
and for which they have no explanation. These
facts are: that the earth tends to wobble on its
axis and that the South polar ice cap is growing.
Brown's theory sees this growing ice cap, together with the earth's wobble as a disastrous mix
that could lead to the earth toppling over. The
earth could, of course, adjust itself but human
civilization would, in the meantime, be lost
under water.

Brown also hypothesized that pole shifts have taken place two hundred times in the last six hundred thousand years. The next pole shift is dangerously close - some think by the year 2030. The existence of past pole shifts would explain the sudden extinction of dinosaurs and why mammoths and other animals have been found frozen in Arctic regions where they never would have been able to survive in the present climate. The pole shift theory explains the prophesies of ruin for the earth existing in American Indian and East Indian cultures and in the Bible. The pole shift theory also has much support from **psychics** and **channels**. See also **earth changes**.

Positive - 1) come to mean - The qualitative assessment from a particular point of view; something happy or pleasant; to one's benefit. 2) The "positively" charged North magnetic pole of any system such as a battery or the earth. 3) In the ancient eastern religions, the male aspect of the universe, **yang** (Chinese) and **bindu** (Hindu) concepts. See also **male principle**.

Poverty consciousness - Describes the frame of mind of those who dwell on how little material wealth they have and how little they are likely to have. This limiting frame of mind will often keep people from seeing a brighter future. See also **affirmations, limitations**.

Power objects - With a history in **shamanism**, **witchcraft** and the relics of the Roman Catholic church, the power object seems to have magical qualities which can bring power to the owner.

The power seems to be inherent in the object rather than having been put in or programmed from the outside.   See also **amulet, personal power, talisman**.

Prana - Sanskrit. Usually translated as breath, prana is much more. It is the underlying force of all life and the entire universe. As the **yoga** master B.K.S. Iyengar described it, it is "the hub of the wheel of life." Prana can be thought of as the animating force that is in everything. See also **ch'i, ether, T'ai chi chuan**.

Precognition - The phenomenon of knowing what will happen before it happens. "Pre" meaning before. "Cognition" meaning knowing.

Primal scream - Primal Therapy, developed by Arthur Janov, brings deep rooted emotions to the surface. When these painful emotions come up, the patient is encouraged to let the emotions out in the form of a scream. The patient is then better able to continue this very structured, guided healing process. The scream is literally like letting the steam out of a boiling kettle all at once. Some people have borrowed the "scream" from Janov's body of work. When things feel out of control or frustrating they might drive off to a deserted place and scream. They can then go back about their business feeling some relief.

Process - buzzword. 1) An individual's life. The soul's place and/or level of progress on the **evolutionary spiral** at any given time. 2) What actually happens to an individual in terms of change during a specific therapeutic approach or throughout life. 3) How an individual deals with the circumstances attached to events that come up during therapy or with life in general. "How I process . . ."

Processing - buzzword. Similar to "thinking through" something. "Processing," however, involves the emotions as well as the mind. For example, "I don't have anything to say at this time, I am still processing what we talked about last week."

Program - This term, borrowed from the field of computers, refers 1) to a method of imprinting a thought on a **crystal** or other object through **intent**, a focusing of a thought on the object for a particular purpose, or 2) to the use of a similar technique on oneself or another to prepare for a particular objective.

   For example, to be "programmed for success." This is an active, conscious process not to be confused with brainwashing or **hypnosis**.

Protect, protection - buzzword. 1) Describes the technique of calling in **guides** or sending out **etheric lines** into the Supreme Intelligence. Also refers to the creation of a bubble of white or colored **light** around an individual or situation. 2) The act of creating a grid or field of protection around an individual or object. 3) Sending protection to oneself or another can be as simple as thinking positive thoughts, thoughts of strength. This protection exists **"on all levels,"** physical and non-physical, and **protects** from undesirable influences at all levels. See also **amulet, create, surround in (white) light, talisman.**

Psychic - A person who is either born with or develops many gifts or talents in the areas of **ESP, clairvoyance,** communication with the **spirit world,** abilities to read the human **aura** and uses these special skills as a **healer** or **reader**.

Psychosomatic connection - The link between the mind (psyche) and the body (soma). The idea that this connection exists is not new, but it has really taken hold in the New Age. The state of health of the mind is dependent on and affects the state of health of the body, and vice-versa. There is an unbreakable bond between the two. Treating both mind (the intellect and the emotions) and body simultaneously for an illness has been shown to be more effective than focusing on just one of them. See also **holism, holistic health therapies, on all levels.**

Put it out into the universe - buzzphrase. Refers to the process of manifesting or expressing a desire for something. See **manifest** and **give it to the Universe** for a more complete explanation. See also **personal power**.

Pyramids, pyramid power - One of the most celebrated geometric forms of all time. The pyramid is a five sided figure. Four of the five sides are triangles and the fifth, the bottom, is a square. "The" pyramid is the pyramid of Giza in Cairo, Egypt.

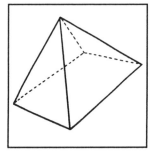

To be effective as a **tool,** a pyramid must adhere to very specific rules of construction. The measurements of the various sides are in strict proportion to each other. The position of the pyramid is also important. One side of the form must be aligned to true north, as is Giza.

The pyramid brings whatever is in or under it closer to its most perfect state. A pyramid can enhance meditation, encourage growth and preserve whatever is inside it. Any material can be used in the construction of a pyramid. Small pyramids sculpted from various minerals are commercially available as are frame-like pyramid shapes made of copper tubing, large enough to sit or sleep under. **Note: The effects of sitting or sleeping under a pyramid can be very powerful. Pyramids should be explored through books or lectures before using them for extended periods of time.**

Today, despite all the research and experimentation, there is only speculation and opinion as to why and how the pyramids were constructed and what might be their uses in the future.

∞ **Q** ∞

Quabalah - Please see **Kabalah.**

Quantum leap, quantum jump - A sudden jump or leap in the level of understanding. Also called an intuitive leap. This type of understanding is non-linear in nature. See also **right-brain, shift**.

Quartz - A **crystal** used for its healing properties and ability to amplify **energy**, especially thought. See also **crystal healing, crystals**.

∞ R ∞

Ramtha - A popular, channeled **entity**. A 35,000 year old man, channeled by J.Z. Knight. See also **channel**.

Reader - 1) A person who understands and uses one or more of the esoteric disciplines or **oracles** such as the **tarot cards** or **astrology**. 2) One who receives previously unknown information in an unusual manner, such as a **psychic** or a **channel**.

Reading - A session with a **reader**. The reading usually provides information and insight into past, present and future lives. It may include information about health and how to improve it, information about **guides** or, if there are specific questions, the reading may focus upon them.

Reason - buzzphrase. Everything happens for a reason. A phrase of comfort when things didn't go the way we hoped or planned or of explanation when something did go exactly as planned. Use of this phrase is based on any one of several ideas: that of the interconnectedness of everything (**holism**); the idea that for every action there is a corresponding reaction (**karma**); or the idea of a preordained destiny, some greater plan that we may not be aware of.

Rebirthing - A technique which simulates the birth process. It is done with the help of a therapist known as a "rebirther." The therapy makes use of deep breathing techniques which help the client release deeply buried emotions thought to have been in place since birth. The birth process can be recreated and changed into a happy and nurturing experience.

Recharge - come to mean - To rest or rejuvenate in order for the life energy or **ch'i** to return to a vital level - physically, mentally and emotionally. The need to recharge indicates that the life energy has been drained by something: responsibilities, the environment in general or other things or people directly involved in the individual's work or surroundings.

The use of the word recharge is interesting in light of the New Age idea that we are dependent upon our charge or **electromagnetic field** or **bio-energy** to be in good shape, in order for us to feel good. See also **aura**.

Reflexology - **A massage** technique based on the concept that there are points on the feet which have a direct relationship to other areas of the body. Stimulation of these points through massage encourages the natural healing process of the body in the area related to that point on the foot. It is also possible to deduce that a particular organ is not functioning at its best if there is tenderness in the corresponding point on the foot. A reflexology session is very relaxing and refreshing and especially good for those who suffer from headaches, sinus congestion or who spend a lot of time standing. See also **Alexander method, bodywork, Rolfing**.

Regression, regress - Please see **past life regression**.

Reich, Wilhelm - (1897 - 1957). Born in Austro-Hungary, Reich was a student and colleague of Sigmund Freud and he made lasting contributions to early psychoanalytic techniques. His innovative contribution was the approach in which the analyst concentrated on the overall character structure in treating a patient rather than on individual symptoms. This important body of work is still used in training psychoanalysts today.

About 1934 his work turned to attempting to quantify orgones, the name he gave to units of cosmic energy. He felt that orgone was the fundamental energy behind all processes of life. He also felt that both mental and physical illness were due to a lack of orgone energy.

His research and study and his invention, the orgone box, or "accumulator," were highly controversial in their day. The accumulator is a box which concentrates cosmic energy, or orgone, from the atmosphere. Upon entering the box, a person receives a high concentration of this orgone into the body.

Reich's work touched upon almost every facet of life and his most beloved interests were infants, their healthy development and the prevention of disease.

The study of orgone, called orgonomy, was continued at Reich's request by Elsworth F. Baker, M.D., who, in 1968, founded the American College of Orgonomy in Princeton, NJ.

Reiki - A therapy which taps into universal life energy. It promotes the natural healing process of the body. Energy is transmitted through the therapist and is applied using a simple hands-on

method. Although we all have ki, the Japanese
word for ch'i or universal life energy, the Reiki
practitioner has been specially trained to access
this high level of universal energy in a focused
manner. Reiki can be used on oneself or shared
with others. The technique can be traced back to
ancient Tibetan origins; however, it was essen-
tially lost until its rediscovery by Dr. Mikao Usui
in Japan approximately 150 years ago.

Reincarnation - An idea, originating in ancient
eastern thought, that we have lived other lives in
the past and when we die, are born again. The
circumstances we are born into are determined
by how we acted in a previous life. See also **Buddhism, energy, Hinduism, incarnation, incarnate, karma**.

Release - buzzword. 1) The process of letting go
of an outmoded pattern; this can involve the
emotions, thoughts or behavior. 2) The process
of a muscle letting go of tension. 3) You can "release" another person by letting that person go
out of your thoughts. The way to do this is to
take a **non-judgmental**, impersonal position with
regard to the other person's behavior, a position
which produces no feelings of ill will. You do
this for the purpose of moving on in your own
life without holding any **negative** or unpleasant
thoughts about the other. It is surmised that
these thoughts can act negatively against the
thinker as well as the one being thought of.
Releasing another from your mind can begin to
break the chain of **karma** between the two of
you. It can also start changing your own individual behavior pattern.

Resonate to, resonate with - To be compatible with another person, place, idea or philosophy.

Retreat - A place, often in a country setting, which offers peace and quiet. Often classes or workshops are offered as are various forms of therapy. There are both spiritual and secular groups who run retreats. What is offered at these retreats varies according to the philosophy of the person or group who **facilitates** the retreat. See also **ashram, workshop**.

Right-brain - 1) The hemisphere of the brain which is believed to control non-linear, intuitive thinking, whereas the left hemisphere is believed to control rational, logical thinking. 2) Someone may call you a "right brained" person, meaning that you have your head in the clouds or like to make decisions based purely upon your feelings. It may also mean that you are very creative. See also **left-brain**.

Rising sign - Please see **ascendant**.

Ritual - A set of actions, words and perhaps attire used in a ceremony, much like a script in a play. A New Age ritual might be borrowed from any one of a number of sources. It might be a modification of a Native American ceremony or a rewritten version of a Christian ceremony. The possibilities are endless. One characteristic of New Age ritual is that, due to the tremendous freedom felt within the New Age community, when a ritual is repeated it might be changed somewhat to meet the needs of the moment. See also **ceremony**.

Rolfing - A technique of very deep muscle massage developed by Ida Rolf. The goal of this kind of massage is to release deep tension in the muscles, mostly around the spine and neck, in order to permit proper skeletal alignment and to relieve postural problems and other muscular tensions and pains. Rolfing also recognizes the role that **body memory** plays. By freeing your muscles, you improve your mental freedom and release unproductive emotions from the past. See also **bodywork, massage.**

Runes - An **oracle** based upon symbols derived from the Viking alphabet. This alphabet was used only for divination, making inscriptions and acquiring spiritual knowledge. Each glyph has a name, a meaning and a sound.

The runes, in a physical sense, are small, flat, tile-like objects with a symbol or glyph on them. To use them for divination, you would select an issue to be worked on and then choose one or more tiles at random. You would then interpret the symbols on the tiles in light of the question. It is also possible to use the runes in a layout similar to **tarot** cards. The runes as presented by Ralph Blum, consist of twenty five symbols. There are other sets of runes, perhaps less commercially available, which use different symbols and fewer tiles.

∞ S ∞

Sacred geometry - Ancient Egypt is said to be the original home of geometry. In ancient Greece, geometry was held sacred by Plato. And Pythagoras considered mathematics and geometry as a symbolic way to express the process of life. Use of this symbolism resulted in physical evidence of the process of life itself. In both Egypt and Greece, the schools of mathematics were mystery schools which looked to geometry and numbers for finding the key to the ultimate mystery, the creation of the world.

Sacred geometry lies not in particular shapes but in the proportion and harmony created within a geometric form. The **pyramid** of Giza is considered sacred in its proportions and so is the "Golden section," which is a ratio of proportion in a line divided a particular way. This ratio is phi, or 1.6180339 .... It has been noted by scholars that phi is present in all kinds of natural forms. Sacred geometry can be incorporated into anything that can be built and is used by some architects today just as it was in ancient Egypt. It is also used in the making of **amulets**. See also **Kabalah**.

Sacred places - Any spot on the planet where visitors feel a heightened sense of spirituality. Sacred places are so called because they affect a great number of people in this special way. Stonehenge in England is recognized by many as being a sacred place as is Lourdes in France, Medjugorje in Yugoslavia and Machu Picchu in Peru, to name just a famous few.

Sage -   1) A very wise person whose experience and judgement sets him or her apart from most others. The sage will use these qualities as well as possible **psychic** powers to help others. 2) As a verb, to sage or to clear.   This is done by lighting some sage (a dried herb), putting the flame out and allowing the smoke from the sage to drift around a room or a person, clearing out any negative energies. The sage can be lit in a small dish or shell (traditionally used by some Native American tribes) or the sage can be wrapped into a bundle called a "**smudge stick**." 3) As a noun, an herb that is used for smudging (see definition 2). Although the sage in your kitchen cupboard can be used to smudge, the herb found there is usually specially cultivated for its flavor and is also ground or crumbled and therefore difficult to light. Other plants are also used in this same manner. See also **cleansing, protect, smudge**.

Saint Germaine - One of many **ascended masters**, Saint Germaine is the teacher of freedom. He teaches of the **I AM** presence that will wash away the discord on earth by purifying and cleansing the earth through individuals who seek his teaching. Saint Germaine's teachings are given today through **channels**. Count Saint Germaine is said to have been born in 1561, and his date of death is given as 1784, although many say he is immortal. From history we learn that he was a Rosicrucian, a **mystic** and a philosopher. He was also an alchemist. Saint Germaine is not a canonized saint, as his name seems to indicate. "Saint" is simply a part of his family name. See also **alchemy, channel**.

Sananda - The name that has been taken by Jesus at this time in history. Sananda is Jesus as he has grown and developed over the last 2000 years. Sananda is **channeled** by many people. He always brings messages of love and encourages us to work with the heart. The unfolding of **unconditional love** on earth is the same work he did as Jesus, the Christ.

Sananda is known also as the first in charge of the **Ashtar Command**. It is said that he is always with **Ashtar** on his space ship. When questioned about his presence on the ship, Sananda has said that it is true, he is with Ashtar, since he lives in everything.

Sanskrit - Now dead, it was the language of the Indo-Aryans of India. Sanskrit is believed to be derived from the fifty basic and primal sounds of the universe - sounds which have been lost to human memory. The Vedas, the spiritual knowledge of **Hinduism**, was written in Sanskrit between 1500 and 1200 B.C.E. Sanskrit continued to be used as the formal or court language till about 400 B.C.E. It survives today in rites of worship and scholarly pursuits.   See also **mantra, OM, sound therapy**.

Scarab - Ancient Egyptian. The Egyptians held the *scarabaeus sacer*, a dung eating beetle, as sacred. The beetle would lay one egg, encase the egg in dung, roll it into a ball and then roll the dung ball into the sun where the warmth would hatch the egg. It is said that the beetle would always roll

the ball from East to West like the Creator rolled the sun across the sky from East to West. The beetle was identified with the God of Creation and the egg ball with the sun.

Egyptians wore a carving or sculpture of the beetle made of various materials to give them the strength of the God of Creation. To insure resurrection, they also buried a scarab with their dead. Often inscriptions are found on the underside of a scarab. Originally, inscriptions from the *Egyptian Book of the Dead* were placed there. Later in history, the scarab was used as a seal, carrying the owner's name. Scarabs continue to be made in Egypt as a popular export item. See also **amulet, talisman.**

Sedona - Sedona, Arizona. Sedona is a small and growing southwestern town in north/central Arizona. Built in "red rock country," Sedona's breathtaking landscape is thought to have many **vortex** areas scattered throughout its canyons and unique, red-as-brick, sandstone rock formations. Sedona has become a gathering place, a Mecca, for many interested in the New Age as well as for tourists winding their way up Oak Creek Canyon to the Grand Canyon. New Agers usually visit the vortex areas which reportedly help them develop **psychic** skills and gain insights into themselves very quickly.

The New Age community in Sedona is very large with several New Age churches and access to **alternative therapies** too numerous to count. There are also **readers** of all types and those interested in **UFO's, ET's** and **government conspiracy.** Sedona has an abundance of **crystal** and New Age book stores.

Self-hypnosis - Similar to **hypnosis**. A state of deep relaxation brought on by oneself in order to reduce stress or change undesired behavior patterns. The technique can be learned from books or from a hypnotherapist. See also **alternative therapies, Introduction**.

Self love - The ability to accept yourself just as you are. Learning self love can be the start of a happier life. It may also be the key to becoming financially secure and completely healthy. To stare into a mirror and say "I love you" is a deceptively simple exercise which can cause profound changes in your attitude toward yourself. It is an exercise made famous by lecturer and writer, Louise Hay.

Participants in the New Age have learned an old truth - if you want the world around you to change, you must first make those changes in yourself. To put it another way, your outside world **mirrors** what is inside you. The New Age has also learned that the **Universe** gives us what we want and expect deep down inside (in the **subconscious** mind), so if we want to be loved by others, we must first love ourselves. See also **affirmations, child within, karma**.

Send it out into the universe - Please see **give it to the universe**.

Sensory deprivation tanks - Also known as **flotation tanks** or samadhi tanks. Please see **flotation therapy**.

Separation - buzzword. Separation generally means becoming divided or detached. This word is used to describe the split between God and humanity. In Judeo-Christian mythology, the division took place in the Garden of Eden but more importantly, it takes place in the heart of every human being. This split or separation is the source of **duality** on our planet. Reuniting God and humanity or realizing that there is no division has been the goal of religion for all time. The moment of realization within every heart that we are all God will be the end of separation and suffering on earth.

God is symbolized by the number one. Separation from God - or God recognizing God - is symbolized by the number two. Duality is also known as polarity and gives us the many opposites in life: up and down, on and off, male and female, hot and cold. See also **denial, female principle, male principle, yang, yin.**

Seth - One of the first channeled beings to become commercially popular. Seth was channeled by Jane Roberts until her death. Since then he has been channeled through John and Dotti McAuliffe.

Shakti - Ancient **Hindu**, Sanskrit. 1) The undifferentiated, latent, silent energy of the universe before creation. Also known as Divine Power or Cosmic Energy. As a result of sound as vibration, Shakti is awakened and in the moment of creation, Shakti splits in two: **bindu,** the male or centrifugal (outward going) force and **nada,** the female or centripetal (inward going) force. With this split **duality** is created. This is a duality in unity, two faces of one unit, not a **separation** as it has come to mean in the West. It is this duality that creates the force of electromagnetism that holds the physical world together in a state of molecular **vibration**. 2) Shakti is considered the **female principle** in nature as expressed in Hindu mythology. Shakti, a Hindu goddess, is the consort to Shiva. 3) Shakti is a name often chosen by women as a **spiritual name**. See also **Hinduism, OM, sound therapy.**

Shaman - Medicine woman or man with a history dating back to the Paleolithic era when the shaman acted as intermediary between human and Spirit for the hunter-gatherer people.

Today we understand the role of the shaman as it survives in the primitive cultures of the Australian aborigines, Native American tribes, Eskimos and the people in remote areas of Mongolia. Shamanic arts can also be learned by westerners.

In addition to being a counselor and teacher, the shaman is one to whom others turn when their needs are of a spiritual nature. Above all, the shaman has his or her own personal path. A shaman is born a shaman, born sensitive to the spiritual world beyond everyday reality. It is the path of the shaman to train and develop this natural sensitivity and to control aspects of this non-ordinary consciousness. Control is sought, not for the sake of having power, but for the purpose of maintaining internal balance while moving between ordinary and non-ordinary consciousness and handling what is encountered in this non-ordinary state of awareness.

The shaman can enter a non-ordinary state at will for the purpose of soul travel (called the shamanic journey) or to perceive things which are ordinarily hidden from others. The shaman usually works at night or in the dark when light does not obscure the inner vision in this dream-like state. This non-ordinary state is usually entered into and helped along by the sound of drums and rattles, singing and dancing and, in some cultures, psychedelic drugs.

Such journeys are to places where strange and ancient creatures live, creatures sometimes friendly and sometimes hostile. The shaman travels with none of the impediments of physical reality and yet feels quite able to move about. This traveling is both similar to and different from **astral travel**. To assist the shaman in the healing work there will be one or more guardian spirits who can be likened to **healing masters** and **guides**. See also **shamanism**.

Shamanism - A way of life dating back to paleo-lithic times and existing in preliterate or primi-tive cultures around the world today. Shaman-ism sees everything as being alive, including things usually considered inanimate, such as this book. Everything has an inherent power. Sha-manism seeks to find the best possible individual relationship between a person and her/his uni-verse. What is sought is balance, which is shown in the physical state as good health.

Shanti - Sanskrit word that translates loosely as "peace." Shanti is a name chosen frequently by women as a **spiritual name**, or taken in a **name change**.

Shiatsu - A healing method with ancient Japa-nese roots. "Shi" means finger and "atsu" means pressure. Shiatsu promotes the flow of ki, the Japanese word for **ch'i**, energy. Shiatsu and **acupressure** are similar as they both involve pressing vital points with the fingers and thumbs to bring relief from health problems. Similar pressure points are used; however, in shiatsu, the therapist will also manipulate various parts of the body. Another major difference is that at the root of shiatsu is the philosophy of **yin** and **yang**. There is a dynamic interplay of yin and yang in the body and the polarity must be kept in balance. At the base of all health problems is an excess of yin or yang in a particular organ or muscle. Shiatsu can work on the human system to either sedate the overly yang state or stimulate the overly yin state. You can learn shiatsu and practice on yourself or seek out a shiatsu practitioner. See also **massage, yin-yang symbol.**

Shift, energy shift, shift in consciousness - Describes a moment when one's understanding of a particular thing or of life itself changes. This does not necessarily take place as a result of a progression of events but can be sudden, instantaneous. See also **quantum leap.**

Simultaneous realities - 1) The notion that past, present and future all happen at the same time. The reason that we perceive time as linear or sequential is that as humans with five senses in the three dimensional world we are only capable of sensing **vibrations** within a limited range. The past and future have different vibrational frequencies. With the cultivation of the "sixth sense" of **psychic** sensitivity, the future and the

past become available. 2) The idea that there are
people who are actually you, living in other realities. For example, there is a "you" who decided
not to do something that you did, such as finish-
ing school. "You" then proceed down a different
path in life, unseen to you as you are to "him" or
"her."   The idea of simultaneous realities is
illustrated in Richard Bach's book *One*, and the
nature of time and time perception are delightfully explored in the time travel adventures of
the "Back to the Future" movies.

Smudging, smudge stick - Of American Indian
origin. By lighting sage, sweet grass, juniper or
a combination of these and then extinguishing
the flame, smoke is created. This smoke is then
used to cleanse or purify or **clear** a person,
object or room by passing the smoke around the
entire surface of the person or object.   When
smudging a room, you allow the smoke to per-
meate the entire room.   It is thought that all
undesirable thoughts or past actions linger as
negative vibrations in rooms, around objects and
in a person's **aura**. The smoke of these particular plants has a purifying action on the undesirable vibrations.   See also **Native American
culture, sage.**

Soul - 1) Your own individual spark of **Spirit**. 2)
Your immortal essence. 3) A discarnate being.

Soul exchange - Please see **walk-in, walk-out**.

Soul group - The one and original **Spirit** breaks
down into smaller and smaller parts, finally
resulting in individual souls. The large cluster

an individual soul comes from is called the soul group. As individuals we may, throughout the course of our lives, meet people we know to be part of our soul group. Although this knowledge is intuitive, it is based on real thoughts, feelings, and common interests. See also **karmic relationship, soulmate, twin flame**.

Soulmate - 1) Another person or soul with whom you are potentially, completely compatible. A soulmate is not always a mate in the usual sense of the word but can manifest in any social relationship such as friend, lover, spouse or child. The relationship between soulmates may not necessarily be a positive one. Soulmates can be enemies in a particular lifetime. The key here is the potential for a strong relationship. 2) come to mean - your ideal mate in life. See also **soul group, twin flame**.

Sound therapy - The use of sound to create balance in an individual. Having roots in the mystical practices of **Hinduism**, **Buddhism** and ancient Egypt, modern sound therapy is as yet highly experimental. The theories are in place but, so far, there is no practice which is widely effective. The goal of sound therapy is balance through alignment of the **chakra** system. This is done by introducing particular frequencies of vibration to the body. Sound is vibration at frequencies between 20 and 20,000 hertz. When the chakra system is in balance, the entire human system is in balance. Sound therapy is often used in combination with light, better known as **color therapy**. See also **New Age music, OM, theory of disease**.

Space case, space cadet - buzzword. A euphemism for people who are generally distracted.

Spirit -   1) When written with a capital "S," Spirit is Supreme Intelligence, the Source, God. 2) When written with a small "s," spirit is a synonym for **soul**. 3) The indestructible, animating energy or intelligence within human, animal, plant and mineral life.

Spirit being - A term describing any one of the many types of **energies** of the spirit world having no material, physical body. These discarnate beings can be anywhere in the hierarchy of the **spirit world**, from high to low, from helper and **guide** to imp and poltergeist. Fortunately, all spirit beings are required to identify themselves honestly when asked.   See also **angel, deva, spirit world beings.**

Spirit guide - A being or **energy** which has no material body, although it has that potential open to it so that it may again **incarnate** on earth if it chooses to do so. A spirit guide is a highly evolved **spirit** who has spent many **incarnations** on the earth and has grown in spirituality and purity. For the spirit guide, earth **lessons** are no longer necessary.

A spirit guide may only communicate when called upon and asked for assistance. The assistance may be in the form of guidance, **protection** or attention to a specific matter. The spirit guide will serve but will never step in without being asked. The spirit guide's purpose is to assist the soul in reaching its most perfect state.   However, understand that if the spirit guide is asked to assist in some way that the guide sees as not for the highest good of the one who is asking, the guide will first ask the individual if this is truly what he or she wants and may even issue a warning that a particular path is not for the highest good but will still help if it is the person's wish.

Spirit teacher - Similar to **spirit guide** but at a higher level in the hierarchy of **spirit beings**. The spirit teacher is not given the opportunity to **incarnate** again. The spirit teacher has learned all the lessons that can be provided on earth and is therefore given the distinction of teacher. The spirit teacher can be asked for advice, similar to the spirit guide, but will give assistance only in the way of knowledge.

Spirit world - 1) The astral and etheric planes. 2) The plane of all discarnate beings and other spirits such as **devas** or **nature spirits**. 3) That which is not of the earth. 4) Thought to be where you go when you die.

Spirit world beings - Also called etheric world beings, this phrase describes all spirits or souls which do not have a physical body. On earth, perhaps due to our patriarchal conditioning, we view this group of beings as a hierarchy.

  Nature spirits are at a rather low level in the hierarchy. **Angels** are at a much higher level. The fact that we as humans assign a particular place in the hierarchy to a type of spirit being does not mean that being is more or less important than other beings. Other **energies** which are part of this world are the spirits waiting to be born and earthbound spirits which haunt houses and people.

Keep in mind that just because an energy is from the **spirit world** it is not necessarily helpful or beneficial to human beings. Any one of this group is commonly and simply called an **entity** or an **energy**. See also **angel, deva, etheric world intelligence, spirit being, surround in (white) light**.

Spiritual growth - buzzword. Often described as the product of New Age workshops and therapies. Spiritual growth is intangible - something to be measured only by the one who is doing the growing. It is knowledge and emotional development gained through some sort of personal experience which changes your outlook on your relationship to self, others and **Spirit**.

Spiritual name - It is traditional in some religions to change your name in order to show a commitment to the spiritual path. In the New Age, this name change can show a similar commitment although you usually don't have to leave society for a convent, monastery or **ashram** as in the more traditional religions.

Some choose as a new name the name of a god or goddess or other **spirit being**. These names may be from the earliest western religions, today called **pagan**, or from ancient Greek, Egyptian, **Buddhist** or **Hindu** religions or from the Bible. The practice of naming a child with a Biblical name is quite common in our society and the idea behind name changes is similar. Being called by such a name makes the qualities of that figure more available to the individual who has chosen the name. In New Age lingo, the name brings the **vibration** into the person. See also **mantra, name changes**.

Star seed, star child, star people - Someone whose origin is another star system or galaxy, meaning that the **spirit** inhabiting the earthly body is originally from somewhere other than earth. Usually this person feels a strong identification with a star system other than our own. Perhaps that soul's first incarnation took place in another star system. Or perhaps during an incarnation in that star system a very important spiritual or karmic lesson occurred, creating a strong bond with that place.

Many feel that the spirit **incarnates** where it must in order to satisfy the law of **karma**, and that there are no boundaries of space. Information of this nature is felt intuitively or is given through a **reader** or **channel**. The star systems most often spoken of are Sirius, the Pleiades and Alpha Centauri.

Stress - Stress has been identified as "the suppressed urge to kick the living daylights out of someone who sorely deserves it." As funny as it sounds, it is not so far from the truth. Stress happens when there is conflict between what is perceived as necessary in a given situation and what one is able to do. Stress can effect our whole life, no matter where it starts: our financial situation, career or personal matters.

Stress has become part of life, especially in the cities. Stress has been proven to have a direct effect on health, being at the root of many headaches, some heart attacks and indirectly, drug addiction, by leading us to relieve stress with unhealthy substances such as alcohol, tobacco and drugs.

We cannot always control the situations life hands us but we can successfully control how we handle those situations. We can learn to manage stress in our lives by applying readily available techniques such as follows: exercise, vacations, change of diet, **massage, hatha yoga,** various types of **meditation, hypnosis** and **biofeedback.**

Subconscious, subconscious mind - The part of the mind which stores the emotions behind and the motivations for our behavior. It also stores memories we may not be aware of in our waking state. The subconscious mind is very powerful. We might even say, it has a mind of its own.

The subconscious mind takes in all information it is exposed to and feeds some of this information to the conscious mind. The subconscious mind is capable of taking in information that the conscious mind does not notice. When the subconscious notes events that are particularly painful, these memories are recorded but may remain inaccessible to or **blocked** from the conscious mind in order to avoid pain. Often when we experience a problem in our lives there are emotions, motivations, learned behavior or a role model in our subconscious mind which are at cross-purposes with our conscious desires.

The subconscious mind is hardly a New Age discovery but many New Age groups and therapies actively work with the subconscious. **Subliminal tapes** can infuse the subconscious with new, positive information as can **affirma-**

tions. Similarly, **hypnosis** can be used to give helpful suggestions to the subconscious mind and to unlock blocked memories in order to get at the source of a life challenge.

Subliminal tapes - Pre-recorded audio and video tapes containing messages not discernible by the conscious mind. Behind the music or sounds of the ocean are messages which can be heard only by the **subconscious** mind.

The messages generally take the form of **affirmations** or **positive** suggestions. Replacing **negative** thoughts with positive ones help you change your attitude about yourself and those around you. When your attitude changes, behavioral changes will most likely follow. In bypassing the conscious mind, which may be resistant to change, and directly appealing to the **subconscious mind**, which rules many habits and emotions, change can be made effortlessly. It is possible that some attitudes are developed in a past life and can never be reached with the conscious mind.

Subliminal tapes are available covering such things as inappropriate anger, smoking, insomnia and issues of sexuality as well as tapes which enable people to remember better, learn more easily, read faster and increase the efficiency of their immune system. See also **affirmations, child within, subconscious mind.**

Subtle bodies - Refers to all the bodies that make up the human **aura**. Please see **aura**.

Sun sign - An **astrological** sign determined by the position of the sun at the moment of birth.

The sun sign is the easiest sign to observe since the sun remains in a constellation for close to one month. Though it does not express the totality of an astrological makeup, the sun sign is extremely important. It helps in understanding the general outlook on life of the one born under that sign. It represents the intellect and relationships to the external world.

Superconscious mind - Part of the **aura**. An energy field of an ethereal nature. Knowledge flows from the **Universe** into the individual consciousness through the superconscious mind. This kind of knowledge is not learned in the usual sense of the word. Rather, it seems to be intuitive or a gut feeling. A **psychic** or a **reader** might get information from the superconscious mind. The superconscious is similar to **collective consciousness** but goes beyond it to higher realms of eternal, universal wisdom.

Surround it/me in (white, or other colored) light - buzzphrase. Repeat this phrase while envisioning **light** surrounding you like a bubble. This bubble of light is for **protection** in a particular situation or can be used daily as a general precaution. It is also used to bring healing, **cleansing** or whatever is needed at any given moment. It is recommended by many that a **healer** create this bubble of protection around himself or herself so that any negativity or illness is not taken on during a therapy session. Colors other than white may also be used. Blue might be used for calmness. Green could be used for healing and red for energy. See also **candles, candle magic, color therapy.**

Synchronicity - A word coined by **Jung**, meaning a meaningful coincidence of any kind. An unexplained phenomenon whereby an idea may arise in different places on the planet at the same time. It may also refer to any two or more events occurring simultaneously and perceived as having some relationship to one another. See also **One Hundredth Monkey**.

Talisman - Although the true meaning of this word has been lost in history, the talisman functions in a manner similar to that of the **amulet**. While the purpose of the amulet is to give protection to the wearer, the talisman may have more than one function. A talisman might represent the completion of a religious ceremony or be an object of remembrance for a person or place. Often "amulet" and "talisman" are used interchangeably and authorities on the subject have trouble making clear distinctions between the two of them.

T'ai Chi Chuan - Ancient Chinese. Created by **Taoist** monks in approximately 1000 B.C.E., commonly called T'ai Chi, T'ai Chi Chuan developed into a martial art and is currently the national exercise of China. T'ai Chi's thirty six slow, dance-like movements harmonize the body with its surroundings, promote body awareness, grace and reduce stress. One who masters T'ai Chi Chuan can then progress to the stage of T'ai Chi, called "push hands" in English, a powerful non-aggressive martial art.

Tantra - An ancient spiritual teaching found in both **Hinduism** and **Buddhism**. Although tantra is generally understood in the West as ritualized sex, there is more to tantra than "maithura." The practice of maithura symbolizes the perfect union of the male and the female in the universe. Ritualized sex has always had a serious role for those who practice tantra. It has been integrated into the tantric view of the universe.

Tantra has its own religious text, the Tantras, which are newer than and separate from the Vedas. It also has its own pantheon of deities. The Tantras are thought to be the true and only scriptures for the **Kali yuga**, the period of time that we are currently in.

Tantra, which makes use of the **yogas**, takes two paths. There is the right hand path, which observes orthodox spiritual practices and the left hand path, the "sinistral" sects, which carry out rituals and practices often seen as horrible and terrifying by westerners. On the left hand path, there are varying degrees of practice. In extreme cults, every spiritual rule is broken, for in the view of tantrism, all acts are regarded as neutral, neither good nor evil in the usual sense. The Hevajra Tantra states that "A wise man should remove the filth of his mind by filth, . . . and as poison can be neutralized by poison, so sin can purge sin." The tantric, one who practices tantra, is encouraged to follow his or her instincts and to do what is pleasurable, for "perfection can be attained by satisfying all one's desires."

Tao, Taoism - Literally, "the way," Tao is the principle of the universe which maintains harmony. It is the ebb and flow of nature. Taoism is developed from an ancient mystical tradition along with **Buddhism**. The founding of Taoism is attributed to Lao Tzu, who is credited with writing the book *Tao Te Ching*, "the way of changes." Taoism views the human as a microcosm and a complete reflection of the universe, the macrocosm. In this manner each object in the universe mirrors every other object in the universe. One who practices Taoism understands the rise and fall, the ebb and flow of nature. The Taoist, being sensitive to the flow of **yin** and **yang**, will always act in harmony with the universe. See also **holism, yin-yang symbol.**

Tarot cards - A deck of 78 cards used as an **oracle** for divination. These cards are divided into two groups: 56 cards divided into four suits called the minor arcana, (which our modern deck of 52 playing cards is modeled after) and 22 cards called the major arcana. The origin of the major arcana is uncertain. Some say that it is derived from the **Kabalah**, an ancient Hebrew text. Others say it was brought from India by Gypsies. And others say it is from China or has origins in ancient Egypt. Tarot has been called "the oldest book known to man." This book is "read" by interpreting the pictures or symbols on the cards. These symbols, like myths, speak a universal language and have a connection to the subconscious mind. The tarot cards can be studied independently of any divination techniques for they represent the many aspects of the human relationship to the universe.

Used as an oracle, the deck of cards is shuffled by the one who has a question in mind and then the cards are laid out on the table by the **reader**. This layout can take one of several forms. In a given layout, the position of each card has a specific meaning and the meaning of each card is interpreted according to its position in the layout. The meaning of the card may also be modified by other cards in the layout.

Telepathy - The phenomenon in which thoughts can be either knowingly or unknowingly sent to or received from another. This **psychic** ability can be either inborn or developed.

Termination (as it relates to **crystals**) - The technical name for the end of the crystal which forms a natural point in an unbroken, fully formed crystal. Because there are many minerals which form crystals and because they all have subtly different structures, it is not possible to describe one type of termination for all crystals. The termination generally makes a point like a many sided pyramid or a many sided pyramid with a flattened tip. The termination is the point of exit for the energy of the crystal. It is possible for a crystal to be **double terminated** or have a point on each end. See also **crystal healing**.

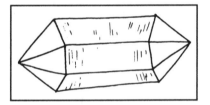

Tesla, Nikola - (1856 - 1943). Born in Yugoslavia. Inventor. Invented and convinced the public of the efficiency and safety of alternating current (a.c.) over direct current (d.c.). Tesla, in alliance with Westinghouse, built the Niagara Falls hydro-electric plant. Holder of over seven hundred patents, Tesla also developed the Tesla coil. This coil has many practical applications today as well as potential applications which might help us to better use electrical power created with non-renewable resources. Tesla died of natural causes in 1943. His personal papers and lab notes were impounded by the U.S.

government and resurfaced in the Tesla Museum in Yugoslavia, years later.

Tesla is much studied by those interested in the history and development of ways to use alternate energy sources in place of non-renewable energy sources such as oil and by those interested in **government conspiracy**.

Theory of Disease - This contribution from the work of Paracelsus (1493 - 1541), the most famous physician of the Middle Ages, still serves as an inspiration today, especially to those who are interested in natural healing. A philosopher, theologian, physician and natural scientist, Paracelsus was concerned with polarity and the fact that, at certain energy levels, opposites attract each other. He also developed theories of **healing with magnets**.

Paracelsus arrived at the conclusion that there were many sources of illness: the **aura**, poisonous substances, individual weaknesses, magical influences and the law of God or **karma**.

Third dimension - The physical world and all its inhabitants. The world that can be sensed by touch, sight, taste, smell and hearing. It can be measured by height, depth and length. It can be described in size, weight, color and texture.

Tibet - A small country high in the Himalayas, Tibet is the home of Tibetan **Buddhism**, which, like Judaism, is both a religion and a way of life. Tibet has undergone tremendous political and religious upheaval in the time since the Chinese takeover. Tibet's religiously sanctioned position of nonviolence is mentioned here as support for

the Tibetans and as an encouragement to seek
information about its past and present. The
world owes much to Tibet because of its contribution to religion, religious art, and philosophy.
Please see the suggested **Reading List**.

Tincture - A common method of preparing an
herb for medicinal purposes. This is a conven-
ient way to take an herb because it is in liquid
form and the doses can be easily adjusted. The
tincture is concentrated and can be absorbed into
the system rapidly. Tinctures are made by placing a powdered herb in a closed container of alcohol for two weeks and then straining out the
residue. Tinctures can also be made with glycer-
ine instead of alcohol.

Tone, toning - The expression of the divine self
through vocalizing. To tone is to sing without
words - to find the notes which "feel right" and
let the personal song take whatever form needs
to be expressed at the moment. Toning can be
done alone or with others. It can be done as a
meditation. It can be used as a way to open a
group meeting. Toning can be used to make an
energy **shift** and therefore can be used as a
healing technique. See also **chanting, mantra.**

Tool - Can refer to: 1) a **crystal**, a **crystal wand**
or other physical objects that **facilitate** a healing
of any kind; or, 2) a therapy or technique that
will **facilitate** a healing.

Trance - An altered state of consciousness used
by a medium, **shaman** or **channel**. A state entered willingly so that a **spirit being** might

speak or work through the channel. The trance state can also give access to information not available in a normal state of waking consciousness. This information may come from a separate **entity** or from the individual's **higher self**. The trance state may look like **hypnosis**, but these are different states used for different purposes. There are several levels of the trance state known as light trance, semi-trance and deep trance.

Transformation - buzzword. Transformation implies a **positive** or welcome change in a person, a change so dramatic that it is noticeable both to the individual and to friends and acquaintances.

Like **evolution**, transformation is a process of learning, growing and changing. Sometimes nothing seems to happen for long periods of time. Then there are times when we learn and grow very fast; the changes we make in how we view ourselves and our world seem to happen in an instant. It is similar to the metamorphosis of a caterpillar into a butterfly.

The inner drive that we experience collectively and individually as an evolutionary process can be described as transformation.

Transition - buzzword. 1) "To make the transition" refers to the transition between life and after-life. Some refer to this transition as "death." 2) Sometimes "the transition" is used in reference to the change we are going through on the earth as living beings, and the change the earth itself is going through; the transition from the **Old Age** to the **New Age**.

Transmission - 1) Communication from **entities** through a **channel**. 2) Passing of information from a teacher to a student - often non-verbally.

Transmutation - come to mean - The process of taking a feeling, idea or thought that is unpleasant or harmful and with the power of the heart or mind, changing it into something positive. In this process, **vibrations** are raised from a lower, more dense rate to a higher, more etheric rate. Transmutation also describes the process that takes place in **alchemy**.   See also **Saint Germaine, transformation.**

Trust the universe - buzzphrase.   Often used when things don't appear to be going very well. When your progress along any path seems **blocked**, the **universe** may be saying that either the time for a particular thing is not right or the situation itself is not suitable. At such times the most appropriate thing to do is wait and trust that the Universe will provide the means and path needed. Trust is faith in the unknown.

Truth, truth within, my truth - Often used to describe one's deepest thoughts and feelings as prompted by an individual's personal perceptions. Personal views and beliefs about reality. Beliefs not necessarily substantiated in external or consensus reality.

Twelve step program - Used as the primary tool for recovery by Alcoholics Anonymous and Alanon.   The twelve steps have led many to recovery through admission of addiction and spiritual awakening.

Twin flame - Twin flames are beings who are opposite to one another in nature, like two sides of the same coin. They are opposites who can be completely compatible as they complement each other perfectly. A lasting relationship with a twin flame is not a certainty because at any given moment, personal choices and decisions may draw us away, rather than to, our twin flame. See also **soulmate**.

∞ U ∞

UFO - come to mean - A space ship, a vehicle from another planet. An acronym for Unidentified Flying Object.

UFOlogy - The study of **UFO**'s. There is a huge volume of material documenting the phenomenon of alien beings and their crafts. UFOlogists, those interested in this information, have been noting and collecting photos and testimony for about forty years. Growing in number and credibility, this unofficial group was originally perceived as a bunch of paranoid crackpots who met to share their mass hallucination. Today, a more open-minded attitude is developing as plausible information in the form of photos and eyewitnesses becomes available. Because of the evidence offered by UFOlogists, the idea of UFO presence on earth is becoming more and more difficult to ignore. See also **ALF, alien, EBE, ET, government conspiracy**.

Unconditional love - Literally, love without condition. To love someone or something regardless of their actions. It is also known as Christ-love because this is the kind of love that Christ preached and has for all people. Unconditional love is likened to the love that a mother has for her children. Known to the Greeks as "agape love," it embraces all creation.

Unconscious - 1) **Subconscious**. 2) buzzword - Describes those with no apparent understanding of their surroundings, no grasp of their own lives, or those who are insensitive to the environment. It might also be said that people like this are "asleep."

Unicorn - A mythological horse-like beast with one horn growing from its forehead. The unicorn has been depicted in paintings and tapestries since ancient times. The one who drinks from the unicorn horn becomes immune to poisons. The unicorn symbolizes power, virility and purity. It is also is a combination of opposites, the representation of union, for the unicorn has a female body and the horn of the male. Like **Pegasus**, the Unicorn can be found on greeting cards, calendars and other gift items available at New Age and other stores. The love of this ever popular creature is not limited to the New Age.

Universe, the Universe - Used as a non-sectarian word for God.

∞ **V** ∞

Validation - 1) Praise and recognition of good points or deeds. Reinforcement of the goodness of actions or thoughts. 2) Agreement between two people on a feeling or impression that something is true as they understand it. These two people "validate" each other's perceptions. See also **acknowledge**.

Vehicle - buzzword. The physical body as the carrier of the **spirit** or **soul**.

Vibration - Vibration is periodic motion. Science has learned through the study of the atom and its particles, the electron, proton, neutron and others, that all matter is made up of particles of energy in constant motion.

It is this energy which gives everything a natural frequency. The frequency of vibration determines the qualities of an object or person. The higher the frequency the faster the vibration. Within our three dimensional world, the highest frequencies are thought, then light, then radio frequencies, sound and matter. Lead carries the lowest frequency.

What has been understood of vibration through modern science and is present in religion through creation myths is that there must be an originating force to cause vibration. What has caused the world to be set into motion is unknown but the search for that cause is the basis of scientific theory and esoteric knowledge.

Vibrational healing, vibrational medicine - A **holistic** healing method which treats the system by giving it specific amounts of particular frequencies of energy. The purpose is to integrate or balance the finer energetic system or **subtle body**. In this healing method, it is assumed that the subtle body is the place where disease begins before it filters into the physical body. Homeopathic remedies, **flower remedies, gem elixirs, crystals, color therapy** and many other therapies that offer "energy work" are all considered vibrational healing modes. The introduction of these specific frequencies to the human system cause what is known in physics as a forced vibration. See also **aura**.

Victim, there are no victims - Given the idea that we all **create** our own reality, it follows that since things don't happen to us randomly, we draw things in life to ourselves, both negative and positive. The idea that we are not victims allows us to take responsibility for bringing difficult situations into our lives rather than blaming someone or something else.

Violet Flame - A concept found in the **I AM** teachings attributed to **Saint Germaine**. Also known as the Violet Consuming Flame and called the Law of Forgiveness. This ray of light is called upon for protection of the emotional and mental bodies in order to carry on in the world unaffected by the negativity and disharmonious thoughts of others. See also **protection**.

Vision quest - 1) From the Native American culture. The vision quest is important in some tribes for those who would enter into a position of high stature in the tribe. The purpose of the quest varies from tribe to tribe. The vision quest brings the knowledge and understanding of the individual's path in life. In some tribes, the vision quest might bring prophecy for the tribe or a spirit guide for the individual. The state of mind which allows these visions can be created in many different ways. They use, for example, sweats (places similar to our modern sauna), rituals and fasting which bring on dehydration resulting in a vision. 2) come to mean - A retreat into nature in order to clarify the purpose of one's life.

Visionary art - Truly the art of the New Age. The visionary artist uses the fine arts to portray dreamlike scenes. This type of artwork is usually very realistic in execution and brings the images to life for the viewer. The images might be of castles within crystals or Pegasus flying in deep space surrounded by spirits or dolphins swimming in air. Although visionary art might be considered by some to be surrealistic in nature, what makes it different from surrealism are the ideas behind the images. Surrealism tends toward the nightmarish while visionary art shows the more positive aspects of our flights of fancy. Also called fantasy art.

Visualize, visualization - To hold an image in the mind. Visualization is done when there is something you would like to have happen or when a change of any kind is desired. Visualization is similar to a controlled daydream. Let's say that you have an injury to your leg; perhaps you are in a cast. You can sit and see a clear picture of yourself running with your dog. Or, if you need a place to live, you can see an image of yourself sitting in a room with your possessions around you. In the first case, the power of thought actually helps stimulate the body's own healing. In the second, the power of focused thought helps you find a home. Visualization is part of the process of **manifestation.**

Volunteer - buzzword. A person who has chosen to **incarnate** at this time to help in raising the vibratory rate of the planet towards healing and peace. Similar to an **avatar.** The difference is that a volunteer many not necessarily be beyond the **lessons** of earth, although such a being will have a special and beneficial purpose for earth and its inhabitants.

Vortex - A place on the planet where there seems to be an increase in the earth's natural energy. These areas are reported to increase the ability of many people to experience **ESP**, to understand themselves better, to communicate with spirit beings and other similar things. The key word here is increase. All traits are accentuated so it follows that if you want to develop psychic skills, going to a vortex should be of help. However, if you are angry, your anger may also be heightened. The information about vortexes has been accumulated mainly from personal experience and as yet there is no scientific corroboration for these experiences. Some say that a vortex is the crossing of two or more **ley lines** creating a power spot. See also **feng-shui, geomancy, Sedona.**

∞ **W** ∞

Walk-in - A soul or spirit which enters a body, most commonly an adult body, for the purpose of performing some higher purpose for the good of the planet. When the spirit enters an adult body, it does not have to go through the process of growing and learning in the usual sense, but can immediately carry out the intended purpose or mission.

It is important to note that the original inhabitant of the body leaves voluntarily. The new spirit does not "take" a body but is made aware of a spirit who wants to leave the physical plane. The original spirit leaves voluntarily and happily and actually may have agreed to this process before birth.

A walk-in may be consciously aware of what has happened although this is not necessarily the case. A walk-in will usually retain the **conscious** memory of the previous spirit but may not feel the same emotional attachments. See also **contract, walk-out**.

Walk-out - The name for a spirit which leaves a body when a **walk-in** enters. This spirit exchange happens voluntarily and the body continues to function undamaged. Frequently, the exchange takes place when the physical body is in some danger, such as during an accident or serious illness.

Wellness - buzzword. Health, the state of being well or whole. See also **affirmations, holism, holistic health therapies**.

Wellness Center - A place where a variety of holistic therapies may be practiced. The choice of wording is to emphasize the goal of being well rather than reinforcing the idea of having a particular ailment or ailments in general. For example, "Wellness Center" may be preferred to "Center for the Treatment of Kidney Disease" or "Center for the Terminally Ill." See also **affirmation, alternative therapies, holism, holistic health therapies, wellness.**

Whales - Whales are some of the most fascinating creatures on earth and the New Age is particularly interested in keeping this little understood mammal from becoming extinct. There is also some question as to the purpose of the whale on earth and its relation to humanity. There are some **channels** who bring us messages from whales as well as messages from **dolphins**. These messages are often about the wealth of life on earth unseen by us on land and the necessity for bringing peace to the earth so that all life forms can continue. See also **dolphins**.

Wicca - True name for **witchcraft**. Please see **witchcraft**.

Witchcraft - Sometimes called **wicca, pagan,** or **neo-pagan**. The practice of witchcraft or paganism has ancient roots. It is enjoying a revival in the New Age. First and most importantly, wicca or witchcraft is not satanism or devil worship. This notion goes back to the burning of "evil witches" in Salem and other parts of the country. Both witchcraft and pagan acquired bad names during the struggle between these ancient reli-

gions and the Judeo-Christian religions for
position as the western world's dominant theo-
logy. Witchcraft is generally associated with
rituals or **ceremonies**, much like many of the
Christian religions. The rituals of wicca are a
way of honoring nature. Witchcraft incorporates
the use of herbal cures and potions. These elixirs are used for healing, not for manipulation
and the casting of evil spells.

Witchcraft is a polytheistic (many gods and
goddesses) religion. In this manner it is similar
to **Hinduism** and **Buddhism**. It has western
European roots, originating mainly in Scotland,
Ireland, Wales, Southern England and Scandina-
via where the most complete information on
these religions has been found. As in most
ancient religions, the woman, the Goddess, is
worshipped as the primal force, the giver and
preserver of life.

Today, the Goddess is again worshipped in
the revived pagan religions. However, the true
emphasis in this religion, when you look beyond
the surface, is on the joining of the male and the
female in life and in spirituality. See also **pagan**.

Work, the work - buzzword. You may "work" on
yourself or you may do "the work." In using a
word which usually means something done for
money, there is recognition that therapy of any
kind, any effort made to improve yourself or
become happier is as valuable as those activities
which are usually called work.

Workshop - buzzword. A course given on any of
a number of subjects. A workshop might be one
day for a few hours. It might be an "intensive"

which takes six hours in one day, or be a whole weekend or week of learning. Workshops are structured to give a finite amount of information about subjects which could be life long pursuits. When taken in a series, they can become more and more advanced. Generally speaking, workshops are a very good way to get introduced to new ideas and new ways of living. **Retreats** often offer workshops and can be a good setting to bring new ideas into one's life.

Yang - Chinese origin. The male aspect of the universe. Relates to the expanding aspects of nature. Other qualities include movement, light, heat, outer space or heaven. Taken to an excess, **yang** can be tight and excessively forceful. See also **male principle**.

Yin - Chinese origin. The female aspect of the universe. Relates to the contracting aspects of nature. Other qualities include passiveness, darkness, cold, earth. Taken to an excess, yin can mean weakness, too loose or spaced out. See also **female principle**.

Yin-Yang symbol - This symbol which is frequently seen on buttons, bumper-stickers and jewelry sold in New Age shops, originated in ancient China. Its true age is unknown.
    Yin is the black tear drop shape and yang is the white. The two joined in a circle symbolize our world of opposites. Notice, however, that the black area contains a white dot and the white area contains a black dot. Within each is the seed of the other. This keeps the world in constant flow, change and balance. This symbol represents the polarized nature of existence as presented in Chinese Taoist thought. See also **anima-animus, Tao**.

Yoga - The origins of yoga are shrouded in the mysteries of time; however, archaeological evidence indicates that yoga began in the Indus Valley about 5000 years ago. Regarded as a "divine science of life," yoga means literally "joining" or "union" and the practice of yoga reunites the individual with pure consciousness.

There are four main paths of yoga which all lead to the same union. These are: karma yoga, the path of action or deed; bhakti yoga, the path of devotion; jnana yoga, the path of knowledge; and raja yoga, the path of physical and mental control. Within these four main paths, there are many "limbs." For example, raja yoga has eight limbs, one of which is **hatha yoga**. This is, among other things, the practice of physical exercise and strengthening postures. Many in the West mistakenly think that hatha yoga is the totality of yoga. Yoga is morality, religion, ways of maintaining health and the science of medicine; virtually a way of life both materially and spiritually.

In the past eighty years or so, teachers from India dedicated to the cause of peace and universal brotherhood have traveled to the United States to teach their yogic wisdom and have reached millions of hearts and minds.

The different forms of yoga are also part of **tantra**, a spiritual path within both **Hinduism** and **Buddhism**. It is the **intent** behind the practice of yoga that determines whether it is considered a right or left hand practice.

Yogi - A man who practices **yoga**.

Yogini - A woman who practices **yoga**.

∞ **Z** ∞

Zen - Japanese. Short for Zen Buddhism. A sect introduced about 1200 B.C.E. As in all Buddhist sects, the goal of Zen is **enlightenment**. Zen Buddhism emphasizes the intuitive experience of the individual rather than reliance on teachings about the experience of enlightenment. Zen recognizes that the rational mind is not able to resolve the deepest mysteries of life and therefore encourages the intuitive mind to search out the answers.

There are two basic schools or techniques employed in Zen. One uses **meditation**. The other uses the contemplation of particular paradoxical questions. These unanswerable questions cause a split between the rational and irrational or intuitive mind. It is thought that this split will lead to the answer of the unanswerable question by finding the "Buddha within," enlightenment. Both schools believe that Zen may lead to enlightenment suddenly, instantaneously. A commonly heard paradoxical question or "koan" is "What is the sound of one hand clapping?" See also **Buddhism, enlightenment**.

Zen out - buzzword. To concentrate with singular purpose to the exclusion of anything else.

Zodiac - The sky is divided into twelve sections which are assigned names or signs as in **astrology**. Knowing what sign you are born under is actually naming what sign of the zodiac or constellation the sun was in when you were born. The twelve signs are: Aries, Taurus, Gemini,

Cancer, Leo, Virgo, Libra, Scorpio, Sagittarius, Capricorn, Aquarius and Pisces. See also **ascendant, astrocartography, moon sign, sun sign**.

∞ READING LIST ∞

Of the many thousands of excellent books available on the New Age, these are but a few suggestions. When you visit your local book store, even if it is not a New Age book store, look in the "Health" section and the "Self-Help" section as well as the "Eastern Philosophy" section. Be sure to visit your local library to browse through similarly labeled sections as well as American Indian studies and the encyclopedia.

Arguelles, Jose. *The Mayan Factor: Path Beyond Technology*. Bear & Co., 1987.

Bach, Richard. *One*. Morrow, 1988; Dell, 1989.

Bates, Brian. *The Way of Wyrd*. Berkley Pub., 1988.

Bradshaw, John. *Healing the Shame that Binds You*. Health Communication Inc., 1988.

Brodeur, Paul. *Currents of Death*. Simon and Schuster, 1989.

Campbell, Joseph and Moyers, Bill. *The Power of Myth*. Doubleday, 1988. Also available on video casette.

Capra, Fritjof. *The Turning Point*. Bantam, 1987.

Carey, Ken. *The Starseed Transmissions*. San Francisco: Harper, 1986.

Castaneda, Carlos. *Teachings of Don Juan: A Yaqui Way of Knowledge*. Also *A Separate Reality*. University of California Press, 1968, 1990.

Cooper, William. *Behold a Pale Horse*. Light Technology Publishing.

Courlander, Harold. *The Fourth World of the Hopis*. University of New Mexico Press, 1987.

De Lubicz, Isha Schwaller. *The Opening of the Way: A Practical Guide to the Mystical Teachings of Ancient Egypt.* Inner Traditions International, 1989.

Dongo, Thomas A. *The Alien Tide!.* Tom Dongo, 1990.

Ferguson, Marilyn. *The Aquarian Conspiracy.* J. P. Tarcher, 1981, Rev. Ed., 1987.

Gold, Gari. *Crystal Energy: Put the Power in the Palm of Your Hand.* Contemporary Books, 1987.

Good, Timothy. *Above Top Secret: The Worldwide UFO Coverup.* William Morrow and Co, 1988; paperback, 1989.

Gyatso, Tenzin - the Fourteenth Dalai Lama of Tibet. *Freedom In Exile: The Autobiography of The Dalai Lama.* San Francisco: Harper Collins, 1991.

Harner, Michael. *Way of the Shaman.* Bantam, 1982, 1990.

Hay, Louise. *You Can Heal Your Life.* Hay House, 1987.

Isaacs, Thelma. *Gemstones, Crystals and Healing.* Lorien House, 1982.

James, T.G. *Ancient Egypt: The Land and its Legacy.* University of Texas Press, 1988.

Keyes, Ken, Jr. *The Hundredth Monkey.* Vision Books, 1987.

Lake, Catherine Ann. *Linking Up.* Donning Company, 1988.

Mann, Nicholas R. *Sedona - Sacred Earth.* Zivah Publishers, 1989.

Neihardt, John, G. *Black Elk Speaks.* University of Nebraska Press, 1988.

Ray, Sondra. *Loving Relationships.* Celestial Arts, 1980.

Rowell, Galen and the Dalai Lama. *My Tibet.* University of California Press, 1990.

Schiegl, Heinz. *Healing Magnetism*. Samuel Weiser Inc., 1987.

Schwarz, Jack. *Human Energy Systems*. Dutton.

Steinman, William S. and Stevens, Wendelle C. *UFO Crash at Aztec* and other limited edition titles are available through: UFO Books, Christine (Stevens) Cox, P.O. Box 1053, 514 First St., Florence, AZ 85232, 1987.

Stone, Merlin. *When God Was a Women*. Harcourt Brace Jovanovich, 1978.

Storm, Hyemeyohsts. *Seven Arrows*. Ballantine, 1985.

Strieber, Whitley. *Communion: A True Story*. Morrow.

Svoboda, Robert E. *Aghora: At the Left Hand of God*. Brotherhood of Life, 1986.

Tompkins, Peter. *Mysteries of the Mexican Pyramids*. Harper Collins, 1987.

Walker, Barbara G. *The Crone: Women of Age, Wisdom and Power*. San Francisco: Harper and Row, 1988.

Waterson, Barbara. *All About the Gods of Egypt*. Facts On File.

Watts, Alan. *The Way of Zen*. Random House, 1989.

West, John Anthony. *Serpent In the Sky: The High Wisdom of Ancient Egypt*. Crown, 1987.

White, John. *Pole Shift*. Third Ed. A.R.E. Press, 1985.

Zukav, Gary. *The Dancing Wu Li Masters: An Overview of the New Physics*. Bantam, 1984.

ZIVAH PUBLISHERS' BOOKS

Zivah Publishers develops and promotes works which speak to those people involved in global and planetary consciousness raising. Our books contain information of spiritual importance as well as being on the leading edge of social and perhaps even political thought. Some of our titles are described below. These books are available through local bookstores everywhere or you may order directly from the publisher using the order form on the last page of this book.

SEDONA - Sacred Earth: Ancient Lore, Modern Myths by Nicholas R. Mann. The author writes "that the Sedona landscape possesses in natural abundance all that was carefully crafted into the ancient temples of the world. It is for this reason that the native peoples of the area called this land sacred and developed mythologies around it which transformed the natural landscape into a potent and symbolic place." Mann provocatively describes Arizona's spectacular Red Rock Country using a combination of Indian mythology, settlers' history, geomancy and natural rock formations capable of stirring the best imagination. 112 pages, photographs & illustrations. Softcover, $10.95
"Nicholas R. Mann does a thorough and provocative investigation of subtle magnetic energy patterns in Sedona . . . " Whole Life Times

PATHWAYS TO YOUR THREE SELVES by Wayne A. Guthrie, D.D. and Bella Karish, D.D. "The fascinating Journey of the Soul through the Field of Consciousness." You are more than just your Conscious Self! *Pathways* clearly explains your three levels of consciousness, assisting you in understanding the "lessons" you are here to learn and bringing about an integration of your Three Selves. This work is unique to these two teachers. 116 pages. Softcover, $8.95.

". . . Its clarity, integrity and genuineness of intent come across so beautifully."   Dr. Brugh Joy,
author of bestseller *Avalanche*

CRYSTAL ENERGY

by Gari Gold. The "secrets" that Indian shamans, Egyptian priests and spiritualists passed down through the ages are shared in this book. Explore your own untapped energies by following the easy exercises for centering personal energies, enhancing communication, simplifying decision making and much more. Clear instructions are given on cleansing and caring for your own personal crystals. Put power in the palm of your hand! Over 60,000 copies sold. 128 pages, illustrations. Softcover, $7.95.

EGYPTIAN YOGA: *The Art of Attunement*

by John Glasser. Everyone might wish for the experience of this author: he "accidentally encountered" a living master of this ancient form of exercise while visiting Egypt several years ago and received a gift of the teaching so tastefully presented here. Physical exercises, breath techniques, theory and meditations are detailed clearly. Information for an in-depth spiritual practice is included throughout the book. This unique form of yoga balances body, mind and spirit for attuning with the natural flow of harmony and creative energy. 256 pages. Original illustrations, Softcover, $14.95.

Order Form

Placing an order:
Check or money order must accompany order. Please remember to calculate shipping charges according to the chart below. Mail the completed order form (or a copy) with your payment to Zivah Publishers at the address below. *Foreign Orders:* Surface shipping takes 2-15 weeks. Checks must be American Express or international checks drawn on a U.S. Bank.

Qty.	Title	Price	Total

	Surface	Air
USA	$1.75 1st item .50 ea. addl.	$3.50 1st item 1.00 ea. addl.
CAN & MEX	$3.00 1st item 1.00 ea. addl.	$4.50 1st item 2.00 ea. addl.
EU	$3.00 1st item 1.00 ea. addl.	$8.50 1st item 3.00 ea. addl.
SO. HEMI	$3.00 1st item 1.00 ea. addl.	$10.00 1st item 5.75 ea. addl.

Subtotal	
Tax	
Shipping	
TOTAL	

Return any book in sale-able condition within 30 days for a prompt and friendly refund.

Name_____

Address_____

_____

City/State/Zip_____

Country/Postcode_____

**Mail to: Zivah Publishers, P.O. Box 13192,
Albuquerque, NM 87192-3192
Thank you for your order.**